One Life

Kate Grenville is an award-winning and bestselling novelist and
one of Australia's best-loved authors. Her works of fiction have
won numerous awards both in Australia and internationally.
The Secret River received the Commonwealth Writers' Prize and
was shortlisted for the Man Booker Prize and the Miles Franklin
Literary Award and *The Idea of Perfection* won the Orange Prize.
Grenville's other novels include *Sarah Thornhill, The Lieutenant,*
Lilian's Story, Dark Places and *Joan Makes History.*

www.kategrenville.com

Also by Kate Grenville

FICTION

Bearded Ladies
Lilian's Story
Dreamhouse
Joan Makes History
Dark Places
The Idea of Perfection
The Secret River
The Lieutenant
Sarah Thornhill

NON-FICTION

The Writing Book
Making Stories (with Sue Woolfe)
Writing from Start to Finish
Searching for the Secret River

MY MOTHER'S STORY

KATE GRENVILLE

CANONGATE

Edinburgh · London

This paperback edition published in Great Britain in 2016
by Canongate Books

First published in Great Britain in 2015 by Canongate Books Ltd,
14 High Street, Edinburgh EH1 1TE

www.canongate.tv

1

First published in Australia in 2015 by The Text Publishing Company,
Swann House, 22 William Street, Melbourne Victoria 3000, Australia

British Library Cataloguing-in-Publication Data
A catalogue record for this book is available on
request from the British Library

ISBN 978 1 78211 687 5

Typeset in Golden Cockerel ITC by J & M Typesetting

Printed and bound in Great Britain by Clays Ltd, St Ives plc

For Stephen
and in memory of Christopher
with my love

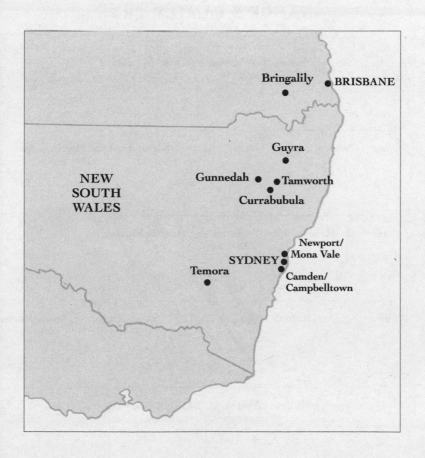

NANCE'S FAMILY TREE

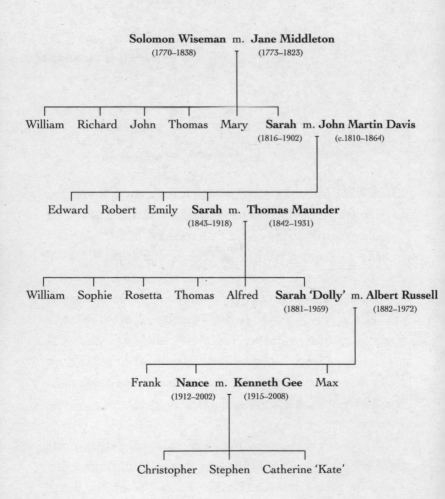

Solomon Wiseman m. **Jane Middleton**
(1770–1838) (1773–1823)

William   Richard   John   Thomas   Mary   **Sarah** m. **John Martin Davis**
(1816–1902)   (c.1810–1864)

Edward   Robert   Emily   **Sarah** m. **Thomas Maunder**
(1843–1918)   (1842–1931)

William   Sophie   Rosetta   Thomas   Alfred   **Sarah 'Dolly'** m. **Albert Russell**
(1881–1959)   (1882–1972)

Frank   **Nance** m. **Kenneth Gee**   Max
(1912–2002)   (1915–2008)

Christopher   Stephen   Catherine 'Kate'

PROLOGUE

AFTER MY mother died in 2002 it took me a few years to get out all the papers she'd left and look through them. I was afraid it would be a mournful thing to do, but the first exercise book I opened spoke to me as if she was beside me, the warmth and humour of her voice alive still: *I have often thought about writing a book—people do it all the time—it can't be that hard. Up till now I've never had the time or the right pencil but now that I have one foot in the grave it's time to get on with it.* I opened another. There was her workmanlike handwriting saying: *There must be a way of writing a story—I'm going to try this time to write it backwards.*

My mother's many hopeful starts all petered out after a few pages. What she left was a mass of fragments. They often began with the stories about her forebears that she'd heard from her mother. Others were about her childhood. Most were about her adult life, up to her mid-forties. They taper away after that, perhaps because by then she felt less need to look back and try to understand.

She often quoted Socrates' famous maxim: *The unexamined life is not worth living.* That terse judgment stayed with her all her life, shaping her actions and consoling her when things seemed bleak. Her sense of the past and the great sweeps of change she'd seen made her want to record, and to do more than record—to work out how her own individual life was part of the wider world. That was the urge behind the rich patchwork of fragments I was reading.

My mother wasn't the sort of person biographies are usually written about. She wasn't famous, had no public life beyond one letter published in the *Sydney Morning Herald*, did nothing that would ever make the history books. Just the same, I think her story is worth telling.

Not many voices like hers are heard. People of her social class—she was the daughter of a rural working-class couple who became pub-keepers—hardly ever left any record of what they felt and thought and did. They often believed their lives weren't important enough to write down, and in many cases they lacked the literacy and the leisure time to do so. As a result, our picture of the past is skewed towards the top lot. Their written documents are the basis for our histories, the nice things they owned fill our museums, their sonnets and novels shape our imaginations. In the bits and pieces of my mother's written memories, I had a first-hand account of a world largely left out of those histories and museums and about which no sonnets, as far as I know, have been written.

Yet her story represents that of a generation of people whose lives were unimaginably different from the lives of every generation of their families before them. When my mother was born, Australia and New Zealand were the only countries in the world where women had the vote. Free universal education stopped at primary school. Very few women worked outside the home. Only a handful of working-class children went to high school. Even fewer went to university or had professional training. Of those, hardly any were women. Even when they did work for wages, women were paid half a man's salary. There was no organised child care. The only reliable form of contraception was abstinence.

By the time my mother's children were growing up, all that had changed. Two world wars, an economic depression, and a series of social revolutions had changed the lives of hundreds of millions all over the world. Many families would know stories like my mother's about their parents and grandparents. Her story is unusual in some ways, but in other ways it's the archetypal twentieth-century story of the coming of a new world of choices and self-determination.

When Nance talked about her life, she often started five generations before she was born. The point of her story was that it was part of a bigger one.

Solomon Wiseman, her great-great-grandfather, arrived in Australia in 1806. An illiterate lighterman on the Thames, he'd been caught stealing timber and, along with his wife and young son, was transported to New South Wales for the term of his natural life. He quickly got his freedom and 'took up land', as the euphemism goes, on the Hawkesbury River. There's nothing in the record about exactly how he 'took up' that land from the Darug people, but the chances are that he was part of the wave of settler violence against the original Australians.

The stories that have come down about him are unflattering. He was brutal to his convict servants and crooked in business. He's said to have killed his first wife by pushing her over the balcony. When one of his daughters became pregnant to the riding master he's said to have thrown her and the baby out of the house to die. Although he became wealthy, he refused to have his children educated, on the grounds that if he sent them to school they'd be humiliated because of their convict taint.

His daughter Sarah Wiseman married an Irishman, John Martin Davis from Cork. Davis was a free settler, but not a wealthy one. He acquired land in the Hunter Valley and the Liverpool Plains, lost most of it in the depression of the 1840s, and retreated with his wife and children to a small holding at Currabubula Creek, in northern New South Wales, not far from Tamworth, where he started a pub. Paddy Davis's Freemason's Arms, later the Davis Hotel, became a landmark on the stock route to Queensland. The Davises prospered and, as the village of Currabubula grew, they came to own most of it.

Their daughter, another Sarah, married an illiterate Cockney, Thomas Maunder. As a seventeen-year-old he'd been brought out with his family to work on Goonoo Goonoo Station near Currabubula. Goonoo Goonoo was the biggest pastoral estate in the country, run by the Kings, who were descended from one of the early governors. In the family stories Mr King was a hard man to his underlings. Maunder was hardly off the boat, a boy from London who'd probably never seen a sheep, when King made him take three rams—notoriously hard to handle—from Goonoo Goonoo to Quirindi, by himself and without a sheepdog. When Maunder's sister died, Mr King made him dig her grave. Worse than these were the humiliations. If Mr King had to speak to Maunder, he'd say: Stand back, my man, at least two yards. You harbour the flies so!

Thomas Maunder worked hard and made enough money to buy his own small farm near Currabubula. One of his brothers did even better, and made sure his children got the best education the area could offer, at the Tamworth convent. Maunder didn't send his children to school. He kept them home to work as shepherds—children were cheaper than fences. The exception was his youngest, Dolly, born in 1881. As she was reaching school age, one of their neighbours was prosecuted under the new laws for failing to let his children go to school.

Maunder didn't wait to be next and sent Dolly along to Currabubula Public School. Apart from her grandfather Davis, who probably had at least some education, Dolly was the first of her family to know how to read and write.

Currabubula Public School only went up to Grade Six, the end of primary school. Like all the other pupils, Dolly sat in Grade Six doing the same work over and over until she was fourteen, the legal school-leaving age. High school was out of the question. There were only six government high schools in the state and the nearest was two hundred miles away.

When she left school, Dolly wanted to train to be a schoolteacher. Maunder said no. He had enough money to support his daughters until they married. A daughter going to work would shame him. Over his dead body she'd be a teacher!

Dolly fell in love with a local boy, Jim Daly, and would have married him, but he was Catholic and the Maunders were nominal C of E. For a Protestant to marry a Catholic was unthinkable. In any case, Dolly's parents had their eye on someone else.

Albert Russell was born in Currabubula in 1882. He was the illegitimate son of Mary Russell, his father unknown. Like Dolly, he went to Currabubula Public School. When he left at fourteen, he went to work for Dolly's father. He was a big strong man who became a champion shearer. Dolly's mother fancied him as a son-in-law because, she said, no one could cure and slice the bacon the way she liked it except Bert.

Dolly put off marriage for years. Several times she went north to Dorrigo to stay for months on end with a friend from school. Eventually, in 1910, when she was twenty-nine—nearly on the shelf—she had to give in. She and Bert married and set up house on a farm near Gunnedah that Maunder owned, called Rothsay. They worked it as sharecroppers, mostly growing wheat. Bert continued to go away shearing for ready money. A year after they were married, Frank was born.

Frank was nine months old and Bert was away when Dolly found a locked trunk in the shed. She broke it open. Inside were papers about child-support payments that Bert had been making. She recognised the name of the recipient straight away—it was a girl who'd worked for her mother. While Dolly was off at Dorrigo, Bert had been busy with this girl. It was Dolly's mother who'd arranged for the girl and the baby to go away. She'd organised the payments and made Bert keep it a secret. For Dolly that was the worst part, that her mother had tricked her.

When Bert came back there was a tremendous row and he went off again, this time for good. But what could Dolly do, alone on a farm with a baby? She sent word for him to come back. Nine months later, in August 1912, my mother Nance was born.

ONE

THE FIRST memory was of crying too much and being put under her father's arm like a log of wood. He took her outside into the night, the cold struck chill against her face, there was the horse-trough full of water glittering in small moonlight, and her father pushing her head under. The terror of it, the cold black water up her nose, in her throat, choking her. It was only the once, but it was never forgotten.

At Rothsay the heart of the house was a big kitchen with an enormous wooden table and a stove always warm. Her father would leave his boots, heavy with black mud, at the door and pad into the house in his socks. He'd ruffle her hair with a big hard farmer's hand, take her on his knee. Her mother seemed always to be scolding. Always her voice high and angry, a piece of wire cutting through the room. The child's own name came to be an accusation. Nance! Nance!

Outside it was the paddocks, sky everywhere you looked, and a lovely long flowing of days. Sheep in one paddock, cows in another, and the rest ploughed ground with wheat coming up green and tender. Down the hill was the river, the still pool with trees hanging over the bank where a platypus rippled along the surface at dusk, and the place at the end of the pool where the water mumbled over the rocks.

Frank was eighteen months older, like another self, but stronger, faster, cleverer. He killed a snake that would have bitten her, made up stories about pirates, built a cubby for them where they could get away from Dolly. The sounds were different when you were in there, the sun different when it came through the holes and lay along the dirt in bright bars. The peaceful feeling, in there with Frank, safe and quiet. Max appeared after a few years, a new brother. He was only a bundle of clothes with a red-cheeked face, of no interest.

And always the weather like another person, leaning over the household. Rain so thick you couldn't see the shed from the house, and the river turning from a quiet creature lying between its banks to something dimpled and dangerous, rising over the paddocks, the new wheat under the water, trees up to their knees in it and the sheep crying together on a little island. It was frightening, because the grown-ups were frightened. Was the house going to float away? Then the sun blazing again and the water drying up, the river shrinking into a chain of pools, and all the new wheat shrivelling.

Between the floods and the droughts, Nance was five before she saw wheat ready to harvest, each stalk swaying with the weight of the ear, the field rippling gold in the breeze. They woke to a day so hot and still the air was like something solid. All morning a cloud gathered on the horizon and by afternoon it filled the sky, dark with a dangerous green underbelly like a bruise. Then one great blast of wind, and the hail starting all at once, like someone spilling peas out of a colander. Nance saw the white things bouncing off the dirt, the ground writhing under them. Ran out to pick one up, felt them hitting her back, her head, a mean little pain like spite. She picked up a gnarled piece of ice and ran back with it, put it in her mouth, but it tasted of nothing but dirt. Her mother shouting, screaming, for once not at her. Nance could hardly hear her, the roar of the hail on the roof too much even for her mother's scream. Under it the rumble of her father's voice with a note in it she hadn't heard before. Nance looked where they were looking and saw the wheat paddock flinching under the hail, all the stems bowing down, the waving paddock flattening before her eyes into muddy straw.

She and Frank lay that night in their little room listening to their mother and father argue in the kitchen. Seven years! their mother kept shouting. Seven bloody years and not a single bloody bag taken off! Rain or drought or the bloody grasshoppers! Now the bloody hail! Bert rumbling something, Dolly cutting over him. No, Bert, that's it! We're going!

Nance was a week short of her sixth birthday when she and Frank were roused out of bed in the dark. Bert sat her on the edge of the kitchen table and put on her shoes. Then lifted her into the buggy, Frank's arm around her to keep her safe, the cooking pots rattling around in the back, and her mother shouting back towards the house, Goodbye, Rothsay, I hope I never see you again!

They went first to Sydney, to a grocery shop in Wahroonga on the northern outskirts. Bert served in the shop and they lived in the rooms above it, breathing the smell of all the things they sold: tea and bacon, rounds of cheese, boiled sweets, sultanas, biscuits. Adora Cream Wafers! They'd never had them before.

The rich people came down in their carriages. Bert sliced the wire through the cheese, weighed the sugar out into brown paper bags, flipped the rashers of bacon out of the box. He'd be buttering up the customers, Nance heard them laughing along with him. They called him Mr Russell. Oh, Mr Russell, you are a card! She leaned out the window and heard a woman in the quiet street call out to another, Oh, Bert Russell, salt of the earth, isn't he!

Then there was a boarding house, Beach House at Newport, on Sydney's Northern Beaches. It was just Dolly and the children. Bert stayed on in the shop and joined them for the weekends. Newport Public School had stern Mr Barnes, who pounced on Nance to spell *indeed*. It was the strap if you made a mistake, and she couldn't think how to put the letters together, but Frank rescued her, whispering from behind. Well done, Nance, Mr Barnes said, and the praise was sweet, almost as sweet as having a brother as kind as Frank.

Then they were gone, off to the Crown Hotel in Camden, a village a little way south of Sydney. There was another school, but Nance had hardly started before Dolly told her one night that she would be going in the train tomorrow to Currabubula, to stop with her Auntie Rose's family for a while. That was the way her mother was. Restless, irritable, turning from one thing to another and never saying why.

Being without Frank was lonely, but Auntie Rose was kind and loving. She was more a mother to Nance than Dolly had ever been. They sat together on the back step in the sun of a morning and Auntie Rose slipped each hank of Nance's hair through her fingers to be smoothed away into the plait. Auntie Rose was Dolly's older sister. She'd never been to school. She could write her name but that was all. Uncle Ted didn't own any land, he was a labourer, ploughing or shearing on other people's farms.

Auntie Rose worked from before dawn, when she got up to milk the cow, to last thing at night, when she put the yeast bottle by the fire ready for the next day's bread. It would still be dark outside when Nance woke up hearing her riddling out the stove. She'd turn over, coil herself back into the bedclothes. Auntie Rose would come in and wake everyone for school later but there'd be no rousing, no scolding. The kitchen would be warm, the fire busy in the stove, and there'd be a good smell of breakfast cooking.

When they all got home from school Auntie Rose had made the butter, fed the skim milk to the pig, worked in the vegetable garden. She mended everyone's clothes on the Singer, turned sheets sides to middle, made aprons and working clothes. Made her own soap, her own boot polish, saved the feathers from the Sunday-lunch chook to make pillows. She bought hardly anything. Sugar, flour, tea: that was about it. Hair ribbons. Red crepe paper to make a costume when Nance was Little Red Riding Hood at school.

At the weekends the children went cray-bobbing in the creek, played jacks in the dust, fossicked for the broken pieces of china they called chainies. Behind the pub was a good place to find them, where someone long ago must have thrown their rubbish. Nance liked the blue-and-white ones best. It was her great-granny Davis who'd started the pub, so the chainies had probably been her teacups and dinner plates.

The school was one room, with a house at the back where the teacher Mr Keating lived. A playground lumpy with tussocks of grass where they played croquet at lunchtime, smelly privies down the back, and next door a paddock where the children who rode in to school, like little Ernie Ranclaud, tied up their ponies.

In the morning they lined up and Mr Keating marched them into the school with a tune on his fiddle. Every week they had to learn some poetry off by heart.

It was usually the big girls and boys he called on, but there came a day when he pointed to Nance. Luckily she'd learned her verse, stood up in her place, and it was as if the words themselves were taking her by the hand and pulling her along.

> *Though the mills of God grind slowly,*
> *Yet they grind exceeding small;*
> *Though with patience He stands waiting,*
> *With exactness grinds He all.*

Good girl, Nance, Mr Keating said. You spoke that with real understanding.

One afternoon when Nance came home from school Auntie Rose said, Pet, your mother's sent word, she'd like you back home. The words were out of Nance's mouth before she could stop them: Auntie Rose, I wish you were my mother! Auntie Rose went on mixing the pastry, her wrists deft with the knife in the bowl, and when she'd turned the pastry out on the board and flattened it with the heel of her hand she said, Nance dear, you know I'd like that too. But your mum would miss you. She rolled for a minute, picked the pastry up and flipped it, looked across the table at Nance. You know, pet, she loves you.

No, she doesn't, Nance wanted to say. Why does everyone have to pretend?

Auntie Rose rolled again, flipped again. You know, pet, she said, things didn't work out for your mother the way she wanted. Course they don't for most people. Some take it harder than others and your mother's one that takes it hard. She can't help it, pet, is what I'm saying.

There was only the comfortable crackle of the fire in the stove and the little hiss from where the kettle had a leak. Auntie Rose wasn't going to say it, not straight out, but she was telling Nance she knew how difficult Dolly could be. Nance thought, It's all right. It's not just me.

Now come here, pet, Rose said, we'll make some jam tarts. Get the glass, see? Put the edge in the flour so it won't stick.

She took Nance's hand, smoothed it over the pastry, so cool and silky. When you're an old lady like me, she said, with children of your own, you'll show them how to make a jam tart and you'll say, My dear old Auntie Rose who loved me so much, she was the one showed me this.

Nance would have liked to take her chainies back to Sydney, but knew her mother would pounce on them. *What's this rubbish!* She took them across the creek to a fold in the rocks that made a little hidden place where the rain never reached. One day she'd come back and they'd be there.

While she'd been gone, her parents had moved again, left the Crown and taken over the Federal in Campbelltown, a township not far from Camden. Nance had hardly got used to the Campbelltown school before they were off to the Queensland Hotel in Temora, in the wheat belt in the south of the state. It was the grandest pub they'd had.

In the middle of town, with carpet on the stairs and a chandelier in the dining room. Dolly sat behind the till in the red velvet she was partial to. Mrs Russell from the Queensland Hotel, that was something!

The time apart had made Nance and Frank awkward with each other. He was a boy now, playing boys' games with other boys. They were still good mates, but not the one person, the way they'd been before, and Temora Public School was big enough for them to be in different classes.

Nance was nine. Temora was the sixth time she'd been the new girl. Six times she'd been out of step in class: at the last school they might have already done the Rivers of Europe, and here they hadn't started it. For a while she'd be top of the class. But at the last school they might not have got up to Kings and Queens of England, 1066 to the Present Day, and here it was over and done with, and she'd missed it. At lunchtime being the new girl was lonely, unwrapping your lunch and chewing away as if you didn't need company. She knew now that you didn't wait to be asked. Wander over when they got out the skipping rope, join the line as if she'd always been there.

Somewhere between the schools she'd missed Long Division and Lowest Common Denominator, but she was a good reader. She liked poetry best.

> There was movement at the station, for the word had
>   passed around
> That the colt from old Regret had got away.

At home they had a Bible and an old red Prayer Book. Bert had a few Westerns beside his bed and Dolly had *Ripley's Believe It or Not!* and every morning the paperboy delivered the *Temora Independent*. Always a big headline with a photo: 'Level Crossing Tragedy', and there was the car on the tracks crumpled up like paper. 'Demented Russian Holds Up Train', a small dark man in handcuffs beside Constable Cassidy caught with his mouth open.

The strain behind every day was Dolly and Bert arguing, never in front of the customers but in the bar after they'd closed up. One evening Nance crept down in her nightie to listen. She could hear her mother going on and on. Not the words but the tone, that scorch. Suddenly Dolly came out, slamming the door behind her, her face crooked with feeling. She caught Nance on the bottom step.

Your father's a rotten bugger of a man, she said. I might as well be dead.

Don't say that, Mum, Nance said. You've still got us.

Oh, Dolly cried, you children! You children don't matter!

Then they were moving again. Frank told her it was because of Benni, the nursemaid who looked after them. Benni was half Chinese, that golden skin. Her mother was ordinary Australian, was how Benni put it. That makes me betwixt and between, she said. Not like you kids, true blue. She had a lovely smile. Frank said, I think Dad's on with Benni. Nance didn't understand. How do you mean, she said. I've seen him, Frank said. Coming out of her room in the night.

Bert and Dolly and Max went to Beckom, a one-horse town twenty miles away. Dolly said the school there was no good, so Frank and Nance stayed behind in Temora. Frank was boarded with Miss St Smith, who took the photos for the *Independent*. Nance was left with the dressmaker who made Dolly her red velvet jackets.

Miss Medway lived with her mother in a little poky house on the edge of town. They were strict Catholics and strict in every other way too. Starting with the moment Nance put her bag on the bed in the sleepout at the back of the Medways' house, it was awful. Miss Medway whipped the bag off the bed. Don't ever do that again, Nance, she said. You'll soil the cover. Her shoes had to be lined up exactly under the bed. In the wardrobe all the hangers had to face the same way. The Medways even had a special way of rolling the socks.

Everything was about your immortal soul and there was grace at every meal and no meat on Friday. There was a Jesus hanging over every bed and He was there again in the corner of the parlour, with a shelf underneath for a candle and a dried-up cross from Palm Sunday. Nance had to go with Miss and Mrs Medway to mass. When it was time for Holy Sacrament everyone glanced at her sitting in her pew with a little sympathetic smile that said, Poor thing, not a Catholic?

Nance was always out of step and Miss Medway or her mother always correcting her. They never hit her. It was the feeling of being watched every moment and worrying that you were breaking one of the rules that was so suffocating. A few times when she'd done something wrong she tried fibbing. That meant a lecture from Miss Medway about what a wicked sin it was to tell a lie. She sat looking at Jesus all through Miss Medway's lectures. The first few times she was frightened but after a while she thought, Go on, Jesus. Strike me dead.

Now she and Frank became strangers. The playground was divided into the boys' part and the girls' part, and when they caught each other's eye across the painted line she'd see Frank's face go wooden and her own face stiffened instead of smiling. It was as if they both felt they'd get into trouble if they showed they knew each other.

Frank never came to visit her at the Medways' and Nance only went once to Miss St Smith's house, when Dolly wanted photographs of her and Frank. Nance was nine, Frank was ten. Miss St Smith was waiting with Frank on the verandah. Her house was in the good part of town and she was a big confident woman in an expensive-looking pale-blue costume. She had that well-brought-up loud way of speaking. Come along, children, she said. None of those long faces! Frank dear, buck up, won't you? And Nancy, I'll thank you to give me a better smile than that!

The only place she could go to be unhappy in peace was the woodheap. She'd sit there in the dusk, the chooks murmuring around her feet. People were always going on about orphans, she thought. How awful it was for them.

She thought it would be good to be an orphan. At least you'd have the other orphans. And it wouldn't be your fault that your parents didn't love you, because they'd be dead. But why didn't her parents love her? She knew she must be lovable because Auntie Rose loved her, and Frank loved her, even though they'd lost the knack of talking together. Her parents should love her, because parents were supposed to love their children. Instead, she was nothing but a nuisance to them.

She sat on until the chooks gave up waiting for her and put themselves to bed. There was no reason why anything would ever change. Oh, she thought, all my life is wasted!

When she went to Beckom for the next holiday, Bert and Dolly were packing up again. Off to Sydney, her father said. The Botany View in Newtown. Lowered his voice to what he must have thought was a whisper. Been punished long enough, he said and winked.

Dolly was full of how wonderful the Botany View was going to be. It was near the brickworks, thronged with thirsty workers every lunchtime. No house trade, no night work, easy to run. The place would be a gold mine. It was the same story: this time everything would be perfect.

Oh, what a silly thing I was, Nance thought. Sitting on the woodheap thinking it would be forever!

Then it turned out that Newtown was an *unsavoury quarter*. Nance would stay on with the Medways. This time she'd be on her own in Temora, because Frank would be boarding at Newington College in Stanmore. Max would go to Newtown Public.

When the school year ended she packed her bag to go home for the Christmas holidays. She went out and waited for Bert on the porch. She was ready too early, Miss Medway kept trying to make her come in out of the heat, but she perched on her case watching down the road. And there he was, a big man in a suit she'd never seen before, his familiar face, and the voice she knew. Well, there you are, Nance! His hand on the gate, his smile turned up to her. Something opened in her and the pent-up tears flooded out.

Oh, things could be so simple! It was nothing more than a matter of Bert saying to Miss Medway, I'll be taking Nance back with me. That was all it took.

They all looked different, city folk now. Max loved the public school, the kick-about with a ball at lunchtime. The *unsavoury quarter* business didn't worry him.

Frank hated Newington. The other boys were snobs, he said. A boy told me I was from the sort of family that had to buy their own silver, he said. Would you know what that meant, Nance?

Of course she didn't.

Means it's supposed to have come down in the family, he said. If you have to buy it, you're not good enough.

Nance didn't care what Bert and Dolly would do with her. Anything was better than the Medways'. That was until they told her. She was going to a convent in another suburb. She'd be a term boarder there, just come home for the holidays.

She was one of two non-Catholics in her class. In the whole school there were only a dozen. When everyone else did the Legion of Mary the non-Catholics had to do their sampler, and when the rest went away for a week on Retreat they had to stay behind with one of the Sisters. Oh, it was wonderful, the others said when they came back. But you wouldn't understand.

Nance wished she could be a Catholic. She'd be happy to believe whatever you had to. Imagine, though, going home and telling Dolly! Not that her mother was religious, but if you were a Protestant you didn't turn.

Up in the dormitory you had to get dressed and undressed under your nightie, otherwise it might be an Occasion of Sin. At the end of the room there was a life-sized statue of Mary holding Baby Jesus. Wherever you stood she was looking somewhere else.

Once a week Sister passed a slate around the class. You were supposed to write down all the good deeds you'd done during the week, but they had to be Catholic things: Holy Mass, Spiritual Communion, Self-Denial. Nance just passed the slate along to the next girl.

Someone had to come to see her every week because her washing was done at home. She supposed it was to save money but it was one more difference that set her apart. Sometimes Frank was sent, stiff in his Newington uniform, embarrassed by the picture of Jesus pointing to a light shining out of his chest. Other times it was Bert. How's my girl, he boomed, not realising you were supposed to *moderate your voice*. He always brought the same thing: two bars of Old Gold chocolate.

Dad, I'd rather have milk chocolate, she said, speaking quietly to give him the idea.

What's that, pet? Oh, that's all right, Nance, milk next time. But it was always Old Gold, because that was what he liked.

They didn't often have treats at the convent but one Saturday they were to go to a fete at a nearby school. It was a rare privilege to leave the grounds behind the high walls. The trouble was, the day opened wet and stayed wet and the nuns said they wouldn't be going if the rain kept up. The girls spent the morning going in and out of the chapel praying for the rain to stop. Even Nance went in with the others, knelt down the way they did and thought, Please, God, let it stop raining.

Lunchtime came and still it rained. See, Nance said to Maureen, next to her at the table. God's laughing at us.

Maureen said, That's a wicked sinful thing to say, Nance Russell!

Who cares, Nance said. God's not doing anything for us, is He?

Then the surprise: at the end of the meal, Sister stood up and announced that they would all put on their galoshes and macs and get out their umbrellas, because they were going to the fete.

Nance wondered why they'd changed their minds. Then she thought, It's to keep everyone believing. Better to get wet than to grizzle that God didn't answer our prayers.

Oh, what bliss to walk out the big blue gate and along the road where ordinary bustling life was going on! To know that there was still a world out there, and she'd surely get back to it one day.

She'd been at the convent three terms when Dolly and Bert sold the Botany View. They bought a block of flats in Kings Cross and a house in the southern suburb of Cronulla and retired to live off their rents like gentry. They left Nance at the convent. She went to the Cronulla house for the holidays, but it was hard to enjoy because hanging over every day was the knowledge that soon she'd have to go back behind the hated walls.

She'd become a troublemaker. She made the other girls try to prove that God existed. And if He existed, then why hadn't He made the rain stop the day of the fete? She scoffed at the miracles in the Bible and laughed at the plaster saints in the chapel. She had a couple of the girls half convinced. Then someone snitched. She had a frightening interview with Mother Superior: the light behind her so she was a dark silhouette. You are doing the Devil's work, Nance Russell, Mother Superior said. You are sending girls to Hell. God didn't frighten Nance, but Mother Superior did.

That was a Friday, and the next morning Nance went home for a long weekend. She was still shaky from the interview with Mother Superior. She thought she'd got too tough for tears but she was hollowed out behind her brave front. Once she was home she collapsed. She could hear herself howl, the sort of noise an animal might make. They crowded around, touched her and tried to soothe her. Even Dolly tried to give her a bony hug. At last she told them. Mother Superior said she was sending girls to Hell, she said in a voice gone ropy with crying. Dolly boiled up. How dare she! Who did the woman think she was? The insult of it!

On Monday, Bert went to the convent and got Nance's things. He came back furious. He'd just paid the next term's fees and they wouldn't give the money back. I'll stop the bloody cheque, he said, and went straight to the bank, but Mother Superior had already cashed it.

It was a luxury to wake up at home next day with a throat full of razor blades and a shivering that no blankets could warm. Nance lay in her little room in the Cronulla house, hearing the magpies, watching the shadow of the tree move across the wall. At night when she tossed and turned there was a pair of crickets right outside the window that croaked, now one, now the other, now both at once, like a song. She'd never heard anything so clearly, never heard the breeze in the treetops, the way it whispered to you, never seen how a star looked with a branch moving so it winked on, off, on.

TWO

BERT ASKED around and heard about St George Girls' High, one of the government high schools. There weren't many of them and they were hard to get into. You had to be near the top of the Entrance to High School exam and Nance hadn't sat for it, because she'd been at the convent.

Never mind the exam, Nance, Bert said. I'll get you in. He put on his suit and went off. Came home crowing. These spinster-schoolmarm types, he said. Bit of man's charm goes a long way. Not a bad-looking woman, as a matter of fact.

Spinster schoolmarms they might have been, but these teachers were like no women Nance had ever met. At assembly when they sat on the stage in their academic gowns you could see they were all graduates. She hadn't known that women could have university degrees. They were all Miss, because female public servants weren't allowed to be married. But they weren't apologetic old maids. They were forthright and confident, spoke with authority. Miss Barnes, the woman Bert thought he'd charmed, gave speeches at assembly where she quoted Latin and Greek as easily as English. She had a fine way with words. The dragons of twentieth-century life are ignorance, incompetence, slackness and disloyalty, she said. Girls, you must dispel them from your lives!

Nance was used to school being dull. The repetitions, the drilling, the chanting lists, everything boring because it was too easy. At the start she sat up the back giggling and whispering. There was a girl, Claire Gannon, who she could tempt. The teachers saw, but there were no detentions, no canings. If you didn't listen and missed something, it was your loss. When Miss Moore asked Nance what *homely* meant in *David Copperfield* and she said *home-loving*, Miss Moore said dryly, Congratulations, Nance, I can see you're making the most of your education.

The hardest maths Nance had ever done was the seven times table but here Miss Cohen was doing algebra. Miss Cohen drove a car to school. Nance had never seen a woman behind the wheel before. A girl who lived near her said Miss Cohen smoked and wore trousers at home. Miss Cohen made no secret of the fact that she spent her weekends betting at the horse races. Girls, she told them, I'm living proof that there's money to be made in mathematics.

Nance began to see that these teachers didn't treat the girls like underlings to be disciplined or animals to be trained, but as unformed versions of themselves.

It wasn't much fun being the rebel no one cared about. It was more interesting to be part of the class, all those other clever girls doing plays in Latin in bedsheet togas, or debating whether or not It's a Man's World. She made friends and for the first time in her life felt part of things. She even got a warm mention in the school magazine: 'A new girl joined us in midwinter and is already proving herself one of our best scholars.' Nance worked hard and did well. Every term she was promoted. After eighteen months she was about to go into the top class.

She loved living privately, not in a hotel, and loved that the family was together for the first time in years. Max was at Cronulla Public School and Frank came home from Newington every weekend.

Bert got Nance and Max up for school, gave them their porridge, made their school lunches. The lunch embarrassed Nance. Her father didn't seem to know what a school lunch should look like. She longed for egg or cheese sandwiches like the other girls but it was always what he would have liked, a working man's lunch: a cold chop with a couple of tomatoes or a big chunk of strong cheese. The other girls would sit around waiting for her to undo her lunch. At first she thought they were laughing at her, but after a time she realised they'd have liked a cold chop now and then.

The doctors thought Dolly's womb might be at the bottom of her moods and always being off-colour, and she had a hysterectomy. It didn't seem to help. She was in bed a lot of the time. Oh, she was sick. No one knew how she suffered.

Still, she had some good times too. Bert bought a car and she learned to drive, like Miss Cohen. Most Saturdays they'd drive to the races and the children were free to do as they pleased. In winter they took pancake batter in a jar and went into the bush near the house, made a little fire and cooked the batter. Nothing had ever tasted as good, the lemon and sugar running out of the rolled-up pancakes, the smoke easing its way through the leaves, the water that bright wintry blue in glimpses between the trees.

But at home the old tensions were starting up again like a toothache. She tried to hear what Bert and Dolly were arguing about behind the closed door. It was broken bits of sentences but she heard Bert say, You'll have the income from the flats, then something from Dolly she couldn't hear, then Bert again, You can live here and I'll manage. Frank and Max knew something was up too, but the three of them said nothing to each other, as if by ignoring it they could make the trouble go away.

One night Bert and Dolly told the children that they'd bought the Caledonian Hotel in Tamworth. It was the first time they'd bought the freehold of a pub as well as the license. Eighteen thousand pounds. They'd mortgaged everything. We've got the touch, Bert said. Pay off the mortgage in no time.

Tamworth was only ten miles from Currabubula and Nance knew it from staying with Auntie Rose.

She remembered it as a dull and dusty country town. Why Tamworth, do you think, she asked Frank.

It's the salmon-returning thing, he said. You know, going back to the place where they started. Showing everyone how well they've done.

Mrs Trimm had started the Caledonian back in the 1890s and it had always been the top pub in town. Hot and cold water in the bathrooms, a grand piano in the parlour, a lock-up garage. The cheapest room was sixteen shillings a night and a meal there cost four shillings when you could get a good feed at the Greeks' for ninepence.

Bert and Dolly were lucky they'd inherited all the staff from Mrs Trimm, because the two of them were out of their depth. The first week there was a problem with Mrs Chipp who ran the laundry. Dolly had noticed that the starched damask table napkins were ironed only on one side and thought Mrs Chipp was skimping on the job. Marched downstairs to give her a piece of her mind.

Oh, Mrs Russell, didn't you know? Mrs Chipp said. You only iron the napkins on one side, otherwise they'd be slipping off people's laps. It's how it's done in the best houses, Mrs Russell, I assure you.

Dolly was cranky the rest of the day.

Con and Arthur knew everything about the catering trade and ran the dining room perfectly. Quiet men, both of them, each seemed to know what the other was thinking. They were more tactful than Mrs Chipp.

They pretended Dolly knew what a fish knife was and what shape of glass you drank burgundy out of.

In the polo season the bar and dining room were crowded all day with rich people. Honeymooners stayed in the Bridal Suite under a golden taffeta bedspread with a black appliqued crane winding across it. When the famous soprano Florence Austral came through, with maid and manager and accompanist, she sang for the guests in the parlour. Isador Goodman played Chopin and admired the tone of the piano. Jim Anderson and Jack Crawford arrived with a dozen tennis racquets each. Nance was in awe: Wimbledon champions!

Fifty years after Mr King had told Dolly's father to *stand back, my man*, the Kings were still out on Goonoo Goonoo Station, still the local aristocracy. The King girls came up from Sydney for the polo and they loved to scandalise the locals by wearing pants and smoking in the street. Oh, provincial with a capital P, Nance heard one of them say to the other, laughing, tossing her cigarette away without a glance as she got into the car behind the chauffeur.

Some well-to-do Maunder relatives, Dolly's cousins, came to afternoon tea. Nance saw straight away how smooth and polished they were compared with her parents. Those cousins hadn't gone to humble Currabubula Public School and sat in Grade Six until they were old enough to leave. They'd gone to the Dominican Sisters in Tamworth. Hearing their quiet well-spoken voices Nance thought, Is that why Mum kept trying me with the Catholics?

Dolly insisted on giving them a tour of the place. The Bridal Suite, everyone staring at the gold taffeta bedspread. The parlour where Florence Austral had sung. Dolly told them how much it cost to have the piano tuned. How someone had offered her twenty pounds apiece for the firedogs. The Maunder ladies said, Oh really, Dolly. Fancy that. Nance saw that her mother was the only one in the room who wasn't embarrassed.

There were a few Russell relatives too. That was a surprise. Dolly had always said Bert was an only child and his mother was divorced, but here was Uncle Alan. He was a bookie, had a strong voice that filled the bar. His son was another Alan, a tall dark young man with a moustache like a film star and eyes so brown they were almost black. His daughter Rita was a Spanish-looking beauty with pale skin, brown eyes, straight black hair and red lips. Why didn't I get those looks, Nance thought.

Bert was a man arrived at his dream. New dark suit, a lovely piece of cloth. He served in the bar, but there were plenty of workers to take over when he wanted to spend the afternoon in one of the big armchairs with a Western, or out in the backyard with the magpie he was teaching to come back to his fist.

Frank had grown into a tall young man. Nance thought him handsome, but Frank hated his big ears and kept to the side of family photos. He was out at Uncle Willie's being a kind of jackaroo, because he wanted nothing more than to go on the land. Max was now a term boarder at a fancy school in nearby Armidale. He got on with the rich boys in a way Frank never had, because he was good at running, boxing, anything to do with a ball. Nance missed her friends from St George Girls' High, but having everyone contented for once—they even had a dog, like a proper family!—made up for a lot.

Tamworth High was another government school and Nance thought it would be like St George, except with boys. She felt the difference, though, from the first day. It was back to classes that were too easy. No more algebra, no more plays in Latin. No one was too fussy about things like what *homely* meant. If you got the general drift, that was good enough. Most of the students couldn't wait to leave. Every week another pupil in Nance's class turned fourteen and there was another empty desk.

Being with boys gave the classroom a heavy unsettled feeling, like an undertow. Most of the teachers were men, and if you were on the girls' side of the room it was hard to catch their eye. They think we're all just going to get married, Una said. Don't want to waste their time on us. The undertow could turn nasty if any of the girls beat the boys in a test.

Most of the teachers were fresh out of Teachers' College, working through their country posting so they could apply for a transfer to Sydney. They didn't know how to keep order. The new French teacher was full of innocent enthusiasm. She came in the first day and wrote on the board: *With Every Language Learned, Man Gains a Soul*. Some boy up the back guffawed. The teacher only lasted two weeks, ran out of class in tears one day and never came back.

Esme told Nance there was no point in learning French, anyway. None of them was going to go to France, and if a French person came to Tamworth they could bloody well speak English. Still, the idea that you could gain a soul stayed with Nance. When it was her turn to read out a sentence in French, she felt her face changing around the new sounds. She did feel different. It wasn't gaining a soul, exactly, but there was something.

Mr Crisp their English teacher was older and knew how to keep order, even when he was teaching them something as sissy as poetry. *Season of mists and mellow fruitfulness.* Yes, Nance thought, that was autumn. The apple tree in the backyard at the Cally, with the wasps in and out of the rotting windfalls and the sad smell of burning leaves, the low syrupy sun along the stubble of Ison's paddock, the pale morning fog hanging over the Peel. Reading the poem was like having a conversation with this man, even though he was a hundred years dead and had never seen Ison's paddock. He'd given words to ordinary things that they both knew, and turned them into slow beautiful music.

The poem about Chapman's Homer made the class restless. *Bards in fealty to Apollo!* What was that when it was at home? Mr Crisp raised his voice and stared down the ones at the back. Cortez was amazed at seeing the Pacific from a peak in Darien, he explained. But the poem was really about Keats being amazed by a poem.

It was like seeing your reflection in the three-way mirror at home, Nance thought, because here she was, being amazed at a poem written by a man who was amazed at a poem.

When Mr Crisp read poetry out loud, they could hear the little shake in his voice. Esme nudged Nance under the desk and smirked. Nance didn't smirk back. She was astonished at the thought: Mr Crisp was feeling the same thing she did, a tenderness towards these words that had the power to make the world look different. It was like a secret handshake. You weren't the only one.

She was fourteen and it was the Intermediate year. It was easy to be top of the class, coasting along on what she'd learned at St George. She did so well in the exam that she got a prize, a leather-bound, gold-embossed *Poetical Works of John Keats*. Bert and Dolly were proud, but Nance thought more impressed by the quality of the leather than the success in the exam. Dolly riffled the pages so the gilt edges gleamed in an expensive way. Then she wrapped it in brown paper to keep it nice and put it in the glass-fronted bookcase.

The day after Speech Day, Mr Crisp came to the Cally and talked with Dolly in the Ladies' Lounge. Nance hung over the banister, right above them. She could see the bald spot on Mr Crisp's head and Dolly's crooked part. She heard Mr Crisp say, Mrs Russell, it would be an absolute tragedy if she doesn't go on. She thought then she'd hear her mother's voice going high and indignant but Mr Crisp kept talking, his voice a coaxing up-and-down, like a man breaking in a horse, Nance thought. A credit to you, she heard. You and Mr Russell both.

Nance supposed going on to the Leaving would be all right. She didn't know what she wanted, but she knew it wasn't what Esme and Lois and the others were going to do: leave school and help at home or get a job in a shop, till someone came along to marry them. She'd be the first person in her family to stay at school for so long. Frank had done the Intermediate, like her, but he didn't want to go on. Max was no scholar, didn't even want to do the Intermediate.

Nance knew she was never going to be beautiful, but once she knew not to do too well in class the boys liked her. She was lively, ready for a bit of fun, and she was exotic, the girl from the city. Wade Watson walked her home, Ray Brawne held her hand in the pictures, Tom Vidler kissed her after a dance. A handsomer boy than Tom Vidler or a bolder one than Ray Brawne might have got further. She didn't know if she was glad or sorry they didn't try. She'd have said no. Not that she thought it was wicked. It was that there was no way not to have a baby. She didn't want to be hustled into marrying any of these boys.

In summer they'd make up a party, half a dozen boys and girls, with Bert along to make it all right, and go down to the swimming hole. She loved the hot air hanging under the trees, the cicadas boring away into the afternoon, the silky feel of the water. She'd duck right under and swim along through the tea-coloured water, seeing the rounded stones and the little fish flickering away. Esme and Lois didn't swim, not really, because they wanted to keep their hair dry. They bobbed up and down in the shallow part, only their heads showing. Nance couldn't be bothered. But they'll see, Esme said. You know, the shape of your...you know. Oh, let them! Nance said. Nothing much to see, is there?

A dozen went on to the Leaving at Tamworth High that year: ten boys, plus Una Dowe and Nance Russell. Nance knew that Una was cleverer than she was but old Dowe didn't believe in education for girls and there was no money, so Una was only allowed to go on if she had a job. She had to rush out of school every afternoon to work in the kitchen at the hospital. At least I get a decent feed, she said.

There weren't enough going on to the Leaving to have a choice of subjects. They all did English, Latin, French, Maths, Modern History and Botany. But there was no proper teaching for the senior class. Mr Crisp got them started with *Macbeth* but then his promotion to principal came through and he left for Sydney. The new English teacher was marking time till he retired and his idea of teaching was to make them copy passages while he popped out for a smoke. The Maths teacher left and there was no replacement for six months. They had five French teachers in a year. The Botany teacher was really a History teacher and admitted in a weak moment that he was reading the textbook every night to stay a page ahead of the class.

In the final year everyone put their names down for a Teachers' College scholarship. Nance didn't know if she wanted to be a teacher, but for a girl there was only that or nursing. She thought Dolly would be pleased but she exploded. Over her dead body Nance was going to be a teacher! She didn't say what she did want for her daughter, and Nance didn't ask. You didn't argue with Dolly when she had one of her rages on.

At the Leaving, Nance got five Bs and a Lower Pass in Botany. That meant she'd matriculated, though barely. The university would accept her. She'd have liked to go, study History and English and more French. But what was the point of thinking about it? You couldn't do anything with History and English except teach, and Dolly wouldn't have that.

Una had a place at the Teachers' College, but no scholarship. Have to go nursing, she said, matter-of-fact. That's the way it is. Had my chance.

Dolly had been talking to the pharmacy man from down the road and he'd told her Nance should do pharmacy. It was a real profession, higher up than being a teacher. It was nearly like being a doctor. Everyone called the pharmacist Dr Cohen, and he wore a white coat and had a doctor's grave manner. But medicine was an expensive five-year degree whereas pharmacy was an apprenticeship. Three years of apprenticeship, and a few university courses at the same time. For the daughter of pub-keepers, that put pharmacy up the ladder but not out of reach.

And pharmacy was good for a girl. A woman teacher only got half what a man did, and had to leave if she got married. A woman pharmacist got the same as a man and, if she wanted to go on working after she married, she could.

Nance didn't think she wanted to do pharmacy. Fiddling around with smelly things in bottles, standing in a stuffy shop all day listening to people go on about their bunions. But she could see it was as good as done in Dolly's mind. Dolly got Bert to go down to Sydney to see Dr Pattinson of Washington Soul's, to find out about being an apprentice. Not his offsider, mind, Dolly said. You want something done, you go to the butcher, not the maggots on the block!

He came back saying Washington Soul's didn't take any girl apprentices, though a girl might get in with a small chemist somewhere. Good, Nance thought, that doesn't sound likely. Then a man came to stay at the pub, a commercial traveller in pharmacy lines, silver-tongued, buttering up Mrs Russell. Turned out he knew a man named Stevens in Sydney. Enmore, not far from the university. He was looking for an apprentice, wouldn't mind a girl.

My word, Nance, Bert boomed down the table at her, carving into the leg of mutton. You've fallen on your feet there, my girl!

No! was Nance's thought, but how could she say that with her mother at one end of the table smiling for once, and her father at the other thinking everything was settled? And what better idea did she have to put in its place?

Something else stopped her from saying no: it might turn out all right. Tamworth was a narrow world. When you stood up on the top of the hill behind the town you could feel you knew every single person who lived there. It was as small as that, the grid of streets that naked. Up there with Una and Wade one day she'd declaimed to the warm breeze blowing off the plain:

> Or like stout Cortez when with eagle eyes
> He stared at the Pacific—and all his men
> Looked at each other with a wild surmise—
> Silent, upon a peak in Darien.

The others had laughed, and yes, she'd said it as a joke. There was a private joke behind the public one, though: she meant it. In her own small way she might be like Cortez, and find a world bigger than a dusty country town that rode on the sheep's back.

THREE

BY THE middle of March 1930 Nance's suitcase was under the second bed in the room of her friend from St George, Maggie Glendon, at Bondi. Sydney felt like home. Nance loved the feel of the sea breeze, it was like the best days at Cronulla. Sun glinted off cars and gleamed along tram tracks. Seen from the bustle of Bondi, sleepy old Tamworth was a good place to have left.

The Glendons' flat was round the back of a liver-coloured brick block where the stairs always smelled of potatoes being boiled to death, but that was all right because it was near the beach, and everyone welcomed her. She and Maggie shared a cramped bedroom like sisters. Maggie had had to leave school when her father died. Now she worked in Hosiery at David Jones. She'd have loved to do something more than a dead-end job but there was no money. Mrs Glendon was a timid woman who seemed overwhelmed by widowhood.

Maggie's brother Wal was a cheerful fellow, had left school at fourteen, had a job on the trams.

The first day of lectures Nance got the bus through the city and out to the university, proud of the heavy bag of books over her shoulder. Other than some of her teachers, she'd never known anyone who'd gone to the university, and here she was walking between the sandstone gateposts!

At nine o'clock the professor came into the lecture hall, black gown billowing around his long legs. She opened her notebook, uncapped her pen, and got ready to become a pharmacist.

Botany was more or less familiar: *The Structure of Life Processes in Green Plants, Principles of Classification, Floral Biology*. But Chemistry was a foreign language. *Empirical, Molecular and Structural Formulae. Gravimetric Determination of Phosphoric Acid. The Calibration of Pipettes.*

Among eighty men, six women were doing Chemistry and Botany. They were expected to sit together in the front row. There was a Mavis who she got a bit friendly with, and a clever young woman named Marjorie. She'd have liked to go to lunch with them and ask them what a covalent bond was, but the minute classes were over she had to race for the tram so she'd be at the shop on Enmore Road by one o'clock. Mr Stevens would be at the door with his watch in his hand. He'd tell her again that a master could dismiss an apprentice for tardiness.

The pharmacy was cramped and airless and full of the noise of traffic. The cars roared and beeped, the trams screamed going round into Stanmore Road. The dispensary was a dark corner under the stairs. In rows, with their gilt-lettered labels, the pharmacy bottles looked a bit grand. It was only when you shook the stuff out that you could see it was nothing but dried-up leaves, seeds, gritty stuff like sand. Mr Stevens measured the amounts. Then it was Nance's job to grind them in the mortar and make them into a pill or a cream.

When she wasn't grinding away at the mortar and coughing at the fine powder that floated out, or rolling the pills in sugar, or washing out bottles, Nance had to serve in the shop. The customers frightened her. Half the time she'd never heard of whatever it was they were asking for, let alone where in the shop to find it. Enmore was full of people too poor to go to the doctor and some of them didn't realise Nance had no idea what to do for a nasty chesty cough, or the big red stye on their eyelid. She asked Mr Stevens or Moira, but she felt stupid to be forever pestering them. Then there was the worry of handing someone the wrong package and killing them.

Moira was the apprentice she was replacing. She'd done her Finals but was staying on for a week to show Nance the ropes. At the end of each day they went over the dockets together. That was another worry, if they didn't come out right would she have to make up the shortfall? Some of the things on the dockets were a mystery and finally she asked, What are these FL things?

Oh, Nance, keep your voice down, for heaven's sake, Moira said, and jerked her head to tell Nance to follow her into the back room.

Look, she said, they're french letters, you know anything about them? No, well, they go over the feller's willy. Stop the babies coming.

She laughed. Moira was a coarse sort of person, though not when Mr Stevens was about.

Know what a willy is, do you, Nance? Country girl like you? You'd have seen the bulls and that?

The bulls and the horses were all Nance knew about sex, apart from Tom Vidler's kiss at the Tamworth Memorial Dance.

The fellers are awkward about coming in and asking, Moira said. Needn't be, in my view. I like a feller with a french letter in his back pocket.

Nance felt like an innocent fool, but at least now she understood about the young men who'd come in expecting to be served by Mr Stevens and got her instead. They'd stammer out a request for a comb or a pair of shoelaces. Blushing, mumbling, spilling their change. Later she'd see them lurking outside and when Mr Stevens was behind the counter they'd come in again. They'd wall themselves off from the women with their shoulders and murmur together.

Moira showed Nance the place under the counter where Mr Stevens kept the FLs. There were things for women, too, that you had to know about. Little pieces of sponge with a string that you soaked in vinegar, and the

Housewife's Friend. Kind of a foamy thing you put up yourself, Moira said. Terrible mess on the sheets.

Monday to Friday she got to the shop at one and was there until seven or eight at night. There was another pharmacy next door and they played the game of who could stay open longer. On Saturday and Sunday she had to be at the shop at nine in the morning. At one o'clock she could go home, but she had to be back again at six and stay till whenever the shop closed. Saturday nights were busy, sometimes they didn't close till ten. There was no morning of the week when she could sleep in. No complete day was her own, not even a full afternoon. Her life before pharmacy seemed a mad luxuriousness of time.

For the first weeks her feet ached so she could feel the bones against the floor. At the tram stop there was no seat and there were nights when she sat down to wait on the footpath, feet in the gutter like a tramp. She was past caring.

Eventually her feet got used to it, but she didn't. Did you have a nice day, dear, Mrs Glendon asked every evening. Nance tried to smile, tried to eat her dried-up dinner, too tired to be hungry. Mrs Glendon had left school at fourteen, had never worked outside the home. Nance training to be a pharmacist seemed wonderful to her. How could Nance tell her, It's awful! I don't understand the lectures! And Mr Stevens rouses on me if I'm not back at the shop on time!

Each day she put on the white coat again knowing there was nothing ahead of her but loneliness and exhaustion. She wished she'd never won that prize at the Intermediate, never attracted Mr Crisp's interest, never squeaked that pass at the Leaving. She hated every day, went to sleep with her wrist still tightening around the movement of the pestle, and on the other side of the too-short sleep there was another day like the last one.

By the time Nance was desperate enough to write to Bert and Dolly to tell them how awful it was, it was too late. Something terrible had happened to the stock market in America a while earlier, and now everyone all over the world had lost their money.

She knew from what Dolly and Max wrote that things were bad in Tamworth. No one had the money to buy anything, so shops were closing all along Peel Street. The commercial travellers who had been the backbone of the Cally's income stopped coming. People on properties still came into town but they didn't go to the Cally for the four-shilling dinner, or even to the Greeks'. They brought a sandwich from home. Out at Goonoo Goonoo there was no more polo. The King girls had to wangle jobs at David Jones. At the Cally they'd let go all the staff except Arthur and Con, and they were only kept on because they were willing to work for board and keep.

Thank God you have a job, Nance, her mother wrote. *Lucky we got you in there in time.* Nance knew she was saying, There's nothing for you here.

She wouldn't have known any of it from her father's

letters. Bit of a downturn, that's all, he said. Things are bound to look up any day.

As an apprentice Nance was paid sixteen shillings a week. Bert had paid the first year's university fees in advance and he sent her money every month. Now each cheque was smaller than the last. Still enough for her board, but not much else. Ever since she could remember she'd been able to have plenty of good food, a new dress now and then, the pictures on a Saturday afternoon. Now there was no money for new clothes or shoes and the pictures were a luxury she had to scrimp for. At the Glendons' there was no more butter, only dripping. No more chops, now it was scrag end in a stew and a lot of potatoes. Bacon once a week, the rasher thin enough to see through. Getting the tram from the university to Enmore came to seem an indulgence. She walked, and ate her sandwich on the way, so she hiccupped all afternoon.

But she had a job, no matter how badly paid, and if you had a job you had to hang on to it. Every day she saw long lines of skinny men standing with their heads down outside the church soup kitchens or holding cardboard signs saying they were clean and honest and would do any kind of work. When Mr Stevens needed a delivery boy, the queue of people went down the street, and they were mostly grown men.

In the short days of winter, the wait for the tram home was dark and cold, the wind spiteful as it sliced up Enmore Road. One night she watched the tram light coming towards her, the rails gleaming, the road slick with rain. The trams had been a little adventure in the beginning but now they were the emblem of the hard machine of her days.

I could step out in front of it, she thought. That would put an end to the misery and the loneliness and the feeling that every day would be like this forever. It would hurt, she supposed. But if she was lucky it would all be over in a second.

In the moment she stood with that choice, she was free of everyone else in the world: what her mother wanted, what her father said, what Mrs Glendon thought. It was just her, Nance Russell, alone with eternity. She'd have prayed, if she had the words for a prayer, or believed there was anyone to hear it.

Now more than ever seems it rich to die. They were the words that rose out of memory.

> *Now more than ever seems it rich to die,*
> *To cease upon the midnight with no pain.*

She'd sat in that hot classroom while the blowflies droned against the windows, and listened to Mr Crisp read. *For many a time I have been half in love with easeful Death.* She hadn't known then how you could be half in love with easeful death. Still, the words had lodged in her somewhere, and now they were the words for what she felt. Keats knew how much you could want it all to be over. *The weariness, the fever and the fret.* He'd known, and out of memory his words were speaking to her.

She remembered the shake in Mr Crisp's voice as he read. Now she thought he might have known what it was like to want to die. Everyone who'd ever read that poem and had wanted to die was with her on the Enmore footpath, a spilling crowd of faceless and voiceless people, all bound together by having their feelings put into words. Standing in the dusk watching the great yellow eye of the tram light rushing towards her, she understood why some words were worth binding in leather and handing on. In the darkest hour, all the other humans who'd known dark hours were there with you. They'd been to the dark places before you, and they were with you now.

FOUR

NANCE DIDN'T tell Maggie what she'd been so close
to doing. Didn't even think of telling Mrs Glendon or
Wal. In that moment with eternity she'd touched the
edge of something that lay beyond their world. She could
be dead, and she'd chosen not to be. Her life was hers
now. She was free to do whatever she chose.

She couldn't get away from the pharmacy or the
university, but she could get away from having to pretend
all the time with the Glendons. Moira had told her about
St Margaret's Hostel for Women. It was around the
corner from Stevens' shop. You got a bed in a room you
shared with another woman and they gave you breakfast
and dinner. Twenty-five shillings a week, the same as Bert
was paying Mrs Glendon. She'd save on tram fares, and
get to sleep for a little longer in the morning.

Churchy, you know, Moira warned. Grace at meals,
all that. And you have to go to church of a Sunday.

But not bad people, do their best for you.

The gleam of polished lino and the smell of cabbage at St Margaret's were depressing, and the rules were strict. Just the same, her only regret was that she hadn't moved earlier. She shared a room with Meg Naughton, a girl the same age who was at the Teachers' College. Meg had some frightening ideas. She was an atheist, she told Nance the first night. Best be straight about it, Nance, she said. They can kick me out if they have to, but I won't be a hypocrite. And she was a socialist. Nance knew the word, sort of, and with anyone else she'd have bluffed her way through, but Meg was someone you could ask. Very simple, Meg said. From each according to his ability, to each according to his need. That's my belief. To Nance that sounded fair and sensible, especially when you looked out the window at the world.

But Meg's ideas went in other directions that Nance couldn't follow. Men keep women down, Meg said. Keep us uneducated, keep us poor. Far as I'm concerned, that means marriage is nothing more than legalised prostitution. Nance thought Meg was wrong, but she wondered if that was just because she'd been taken in like all those other women. Meg didn't mind when Nance disagreed, urged her on, in fact, because she loved an argument. The unexamined life is not worth living, she'd say. What if we agreed about everything? We might as well not be alive.

With Barbara from along the hall, Meg and Nance would get the train out to the Blue Mountains or the Hawkesbury River on a Saturday for the afternoon. To get away from the city for a few hours was bliss: to see the bush tossing in a clean sea breeze, smell leaf-mould underfoot, cup your hands and drink from some swift cold creek. Always with an eye on the time, and the shop waiting again at six o'clock, but a reminder that there was a life beyond the pale-green walls of the pharmacy and the grim streets of Enmore. Meg said this was a chance to remember how small a person's life was in nature's big picture.

On Sundays she went to the Glendons' for the family lunch. She knew she should invite Meg, too, her family was at Broken Hill, even further away than Nance's. The trouble was, she knew Mrs Glendon would find Meg's ideas shocking, and Wal wouldn't understand a woman with such firm opinions. It would be too hard to be the go-between juggling the different parts of her life, the old and the new, around the same table.

It was common knowledge among the first years that half of them would fail. Barbara had done Chemistry the year before and helped her, but Nance was sure she'd be one of those failures. Her father's money would have been wasted. So would her year of hell.

The results were pinned up on boards in the quad in late December 1930. At the top of the page there was a note in red ink: *X denotes female student.* The women were all *Miss*, where the men just had their initials. She supposed the men who made up the lists would say they were being polite. But she hated being singled out like that.

She'd passed. Fifty-four in Chemistry, thanks to Barbara. Fifty-eight in Botany. That was a credit. Only two of the other women had passed: Mavis Sherlock and Marjorie Hyder. Marjorie had come within one mark of topping the year in Chemistry. In Botany she was ten marks ahead of the nearest man. They had to give her dux and the Gray Prize. Marjorie was a small quiet woman with a square face that was usually hidden under her hat. Today she was flushed, had pushed her hat back as if to say, Yes, I am Marjorie Hyder!

Nance felt as if the year behind her was a ragged landscape of mountains and valleys she'd trudged through, a road with no rests and no glories. She thought, I got through that. I can get through anything.

She wondered what would have happened if her parents had been unadventurous and contented with their lot. She'd have grown up in Gunnedah, left school at fourteen as they had, married a farmer, had six children. Gone to her grave without knowing how to calibrate a pipette. It would have been a happy enough life, but Meg would call it unexamined. Yes, she wanted to meet someone, get married, have children. She wanted to be happy. But she knew now that she wanted something else as well.

Over Christmas she spent one of her two weeks' annual holiday in Tamworth. The town was quiet. Half the shops were closed. The Cally had a hangdog look. A panel of iron lace had fallen off the verandah and a rusted downpipe had left a long red stain on the side wall. The dining room had an unused musty smell and the laundry was silent. Mrs Chipp was the first to be let go, I bet, Nance thought.

Dolly had become small and sour. She mostly stayed in her room with a headache. Bert tried to be hearty but you could see the cracks. He disappeared for hours at a time. Frank was still out at Uncle Willie's, working for board and keep. Max had left school when the Depression hit. He was helping out in the Cally now, except no help was needed.

It was Max who told Nance that their father was mixed up with some woman living up on Paradise Street. He's, you know, head in the sand, Max said. With the Cally going downhill. She's like an escape for him.

You reckon Mum knows, Nance said.

Reckon she does, Max said.

The woman on Paradise Street made Nance understand her mother for the first time. There'd have been other women, Nance realised now, heaven knew how many. Benni in Temora was one, but every town, every pub, would have had a woman who caught Bert's eye. It was why Dolly was forever wanting to move. Another town, another hotel. All she could do now was retreat to her room. Perhaps Meg was right about marriage.

Nance leaned on the windowsill of her old room, looking up at the washed-out green of the hill behind the town. There was nothing for her here. Only that failing hotel, the cranky mother, the father muddled up with some other woman. If this had ever been any kind of home for her, it wasn't one any longer.

In 1931 Nance started second year. That was Materia Medica, the nuts and bolts of being a pharmacist. From the recipe books of the *British Pharmacopoeia* and *Martindale's*, the students learned the exact ingredients, in Latin, of any medicine a doctor might prescribe. The Australian Pharmaceutical Formulary told you exactly how to make it. The students learned about patent medicines, profitable for the pharmacist but mostly alcohol and sugar. How to know when to send the customer to a doctor. When to let them think you were one. The lecturer told them, If a customer comes in and says, Are you Doctor Jones, simply say, My name is Jones.

The male students could see the finish line in sight, their professional lives waiting for them. Every one of them was ready to look a customer in the eye and say, *My name is Jones.* For the women it was different. They knew that life as a female pharmacist—or *pharmaciste*, as one of the instructors insisted—was going to be no easier than being a female pharmacy student had been. There'd be customers who wouldn't believe you were the pharmacist, who'd go elsewhere rather than trust a woman.

Two other women joined Nance and Mavis and Marjorie. Christina had a sad beaten look. It had taken her two years to squeak through Chemistry and Botany. You couldn't imagine her behind the counter bossing people around. Ada was a friendly Jewish girl who had a knack for thinking up little ditties to remember the hundreds of formulas they had to learn. *If you want the bowels to move to please yers, take rhubarb, ginger and both magnesers.* See, Nance, Ada said. You'll never forget that now, as long as you live.

From working in the shop, Nance already knew about macerating and decocting and the rest of it. Compared to first year, Mat Med was easy. But by the end of winter things were catching up with her. Every day it was the same: the big old alarm clock going off at half-past six, the quick wash in the bathroom down the hall, breakfast, the walk to the pharmacy. If Mr Stevens wasn't there yet, she had to wait outside. A pharmacy couldn't be open unless the registered pharmacist was on the premises. Unlock the door, go into the smell of the closed-up shop: privy and peppermint, and the ghosts of a hundred thousand prescriptions. By the end of the day all the spirit was leached out of her.

Three weeks before the exams, the minister came from St James, as he did every Sunday, to give communion. As soon as he gave the first blessing Nance could hear what a terrible cold he had. She watched him raise the chalice and take a sip.

Two days later she woke up with a piercing headache. Every joint hurt, her eyes felt loose in their sockets, she shivered and sweated. People came and went, some spoke to her, but she was too sick to care. Meg sat with her and sponged her face. Matron pushed a thermometer under her tongue. A hundred and four! Nance heard her say. Best get the doctor.

A few days later she still had a sore throat and a cough and the world had a grey look, as if her eyes were too tired to see in colour, but the headache was mostly gone and her joints had stopped aching. Matron came again with the thermometer. Back to work tomorrow, Miss Russell, she said, as if promising a treat. In the morning Nance could hardly stand and Meg had to help her button her cardigan. Mr Stevens was shocked when he saw her but he didn't send her home. Two weeks later she did the exams.

She only got forty-three in Materia Medica. She'd been too sick to study so it was no more than she deserved, but she'd hoped for a miracle. Here she was, failed, along with poor silly Christina, whose eyes were big with tears and whose lip was trembling. She'd only got twenty-two. That was a definite fail. Nance's mark gave her another chance. She could sit the exam again in March.

She didn't go home at Christmas. She slept and slept, and when she wasn't sleeping she studied. Meg sneaked cups of tea and plates of biscuits up to her, though you weren't allowed to eat or drink in the room. Made the bed for her, did Nance's laundry for her. This is the darkest hour, Nance dear, she kept saying. Don't let them beat you.

In February, Meg had to leave. She'd finished her teacher training and they'd sent her to Lawson in the Blue Mountains. Nance kept going with the study. Back from the pharmacy every night, have tea, get out the books. She had the room to herself. The hostel was cheap, but it was too dear for anyone who didn't have a job. Half the rooms were empty.

At the second attempt she got fifty-eight. That was a credit. She looked at her name on the list but felt nothing, no triumph, no pleasure. Passing was the next thing she'd had to do, and she'd done it. There was no one to celebrate with. She went back to work.

In the third year of the apprenticeship, 1932, there were no more classes, only work in the shop and study for the Pharmacy Board exam at the end of the year. Easier, but lonelier. No one but herself and Mr Stevens all day and into the night. She'd keep the customers talking for the sake of their company.

Then Mr Stevens lost all his money in some wildcat scheme. Came to Nance one day and told her he'd have to sell up. Her first thought was, I'll be out of a job. Whoever bought the business might not want the bother and expense of an apprentice. Let alone a girl. Now that would be unfair! But Mr Stevens surprised her. He'd only sell to someone who'd keep her on till she got her registration. Only right and just, he said. You've been a good little worker, Miss Russell.

The man who bought the business was Charles Gledhill. He didn't mince words. He'd rather not have an apprentice. The minute she was registered, he was sorry, but she'd have to go. He was a pharmacist himself, but he was studying Medicine, so he put in Mr Bennetts to run the place. Mr Bennetts was a Methodist and the first thing he did was throw out all the FLs. She heard him giving the young men the rounds of the kitchen when they came in and asked for them. Your body is a temple, she heard from the dispensary. Mr Bennetts was a lay preacher and had a carrying sort of voice. She'd hear the shop door ping as some poor boob went out red as a beet.

Mr Gledhill came into the pharmacy every Friday night to go over the books with Mr Bennetts. One night he said, Think you could cook up a kettle on the Bunsen, Miss Russell? Parched for a cuppa. She could see Mr Bennetts was scandalised. Making tea on the dispensing equipment! Mr Gledhill was the boss, though, and in the end Mr Bennetts let himself be persuaded to have a cup too, and then Mr Gledhill brought a cup out to Nance in the shop. Mr Bennetts disapproved of that too and she drank her tea as quickly as she could, but thought, Now there's a man with a heart.

Charlie Gledhill was a bright quick chunky fellow, only a few years older than Nance. He had a way of looking you in the eyes and listening when you spoke. A self-made man, she got that feeling, with his sights set on a life bigger than the Enmore Pharmacy.

He liked a laugh. Told her one night about the patient who brought in a script for 'mist. ADT'. It should have been 'mist. APF'—a mixture made up according to the Australian Pharmaceutical Formulary—so Charlie rang the doctor. Oh, the doctor said, the man's a malingerer, I meant give him Any Damn Thing!

One night Charlie asked if Miss Russell would like to come with him and his wife to the pictures on Saturday afternoon, his treat? Win was a pleasant young woman and the pictures were an indulgence Nance couldn't afford often. It became a regular outing, Charlie sitting between Win and Nance, the three of them sharing the big emotions on the screen. When they came out, the harsh light of Enmore Road was an assault after the soft sentimental darkness.

He was using her, she told herself. Getting all that work out of her for sixteen shillings a week. A trip to the pictures was a cheap way to keep her sweet. She was a first-rate pharmacist now, quick and accurate with the dispensing and good with the customers. Mr Bennetts wasn't a welcoming sort of man and all the mothers asked for Miss Russell to look at their boys' spots.

She didn't mind. Charlie Gledhill might be using her, but he was energetic, garrulous, cheerful: a charmer, but not the calculating kind.

The Pharmaceutical Board exam was notoriously hard. It was the last hurdle before you were allowed to start doling out medicine. At the two-hour mark, Nance recognised the trick question that invited you to dispense an overdose of cocaine hydrochloride. She wrote on the paper that the script should be checked with the doctor as the dose prescribed could be fatal. After the exam, when they were all comparing notes, it came out that five of the men had obediently made up a dose that would have killed a customer. They'd all been at the same bench during the exam. Stupid not to see the trick, she thought. Even more stupid to copy the person next to them.

When the results came out in the paper she thought there must have been a mistake. She'd come second in the state. Second! In the whole state! And first was Ada. She'd never known her other name. Ada Belinfante.

She was pleased to see that *Candidates 30, 32, 34, 36 and 38 received no marks in dispensing and in consequence failed the examination.*

There was a ceremony for awarding the Certificate of Registration and the prizes. Last time she'd gone on a stage for a prize she'd been fifteen, and the wife of the Tamworth mayor had been waiting with the leather-bound Keats that had travelled with Nance ever since. *Nancy Isabel Russell.* She set off across the yards of dusty stage separating her from the man from the Pharmaceutical Board. The steps very slow, as in a dream. Each part of the mechanism of walking suddenly strange. The knee must bend, the foot must be pulled into the air so it can be pushed forward. Each leg and each arm operating separately, Nance Russell no longer one thing, *myself,* but a set of parts—legs, arms, feet—with lives of their own.

There was clapping. She could hear it, but it sounded like wind or water, nothing to do with her. The man from the Pharmaceutical Board shook her right hand, put the certificate into her left, smiled his practised smile and used the handshake, like a man leading in a dance, to show her what to do next: keep walking, dear, off the stage.

Being a Registered Pharmacist was a bit of paper with some fancy lettering on it and her name spelled not quite right. More than the bit of paper, she needed a job, and there wasn't one. A pharmacy might need an apprentice, someone who'd work seven days a week for sixteen shillings and a trip to the pictures on a Saturday afternoon. But it didn't need two registered pharmacists. She'd just qualified herself out of a job.

SARAH and Thomas Maunder, about 1890. In her memoirs Nance says, 'Grandfather was a dreadful old martinet I believe and Grandma was very severe. I suppose she'd had a rotten life. It was probably one of those terrible marriages where there was no compatibility and just a lot of hard work, and children, and not much money.'

NANCE'S mother, Dolly, about 1908. 'Mum had a friend in Dorrigo called Minnie Devine and was invited to stay. She saw another world up there and didn't want to come home. She and Minnie Devine thought they could go school-teaching, but Grandfather said over his dead body she'd be a teacher! She never forgot that. No wonder she was always so frustrated.'

TAMWORTH, 1929. From left: Max, Nance, unknown, Maggie Glendon, Frank. 'It was my first encounter with a lot of boys and I liked it. They made a fuss of me because I had come from Sydney and I suppose seemed exotic. Sixty or seventy years ago, you just talked to boys, that was about it. If they kissed you, that was going really a long way'.

DOLLY, 1929. 'My mother had a power over us all that I still find hard to understand. She was not a woman of rational mind at all. She used to get into these fearful rages. I think she was always a little bit funny. Dad always said there was streak of it in the Wisemans'.

DOLLY and Bert Russell on their wedding day, 1910. 'Her mother wrote and said that she had to come home from Dorrigo and marry Dad and in the end she couldn't get out of it. That's why she looks so cranky in her wedding photo. What chance did any of those people have? It's really good to remember how dreadful those times were. For men and women, but much worse for women because they had no redress.'

NANCE'S father, Bert, about 1908. 'Dad was very flashy in his young days. Mum once told me he always had to have the best horse on the place and he kept her in kid gloves. That would be Dad's idea of being up with them. He'd have no idea that that was just being silly.'

FRANK (left) and Nance, about 1914. 'Frank and I were great mates, but one night when the 1914 war was on we were fighting and I said, Well I'm glad I'm not a boy, you'll have to go and fight in the war! He was very angry and said bugger and I—horrible prig that I must have been—told on him and he got into trouble.'

THE Wahroonga grocery. 'Dad often told the story of the rich people around Wahroonga, driving down in their horse and carriage looking for sugar and that kind of thing, and he'd butter himself up to them. He had a nice manner, they thought he was wonderful'.
Reproduced courtesy of the Ku-ring-gai Historical Society.

MAX, Nance and Frank, about 1924. 'Newtown in those days was regarded as an unsavoury quarter as Mum expressed it so I was too delicate to go to a day school there. I was at the convent and used to come home to Newtown in the holidays'.

NANCE and Frank, about 1923. 'Frank and I were boarded out in Temora. He was luckier than I was: he stayed with a very nice woman, the local photographer. But for me they were awful years.'

NANCE, front row, third from right, St George Girls' High School, 1925.
'I went to many different schools, but in the desert of waste amidst the
busy craze to make money I had eighteen months at a magnificent school.
Everything that mattered I learned there.'

THE Russells of the Caledonian, 1927: Nance, Max, Bert, Dolly, unknown. 'It
was the first freehold hotel they'd bought. They mortgaged everything to buy
it. So many lives were changed by that decision. Most people don't have those
choices, but my parents had made money by buying and selling hotels in a
boom time when it was easy if you had the courage to try. Nothing had gone
wrong in the last ten years and they thought it was all their own clever doing.'

THE backyard at the Cally, 1927. From left: Frank, Bert, unknown, Nance, unknown. 'Frank had already made it clear that he would have nothing to do with the hotel. Of course Dad and Mum should have bought a property instead of a hotel, that they could have all worked together.'

PEEL River, 1927. From left: Frank, Esme, Nance, Una, Max, unknown, Bert.

FIVE

BERT MET her at Tamworth station in the old Fiat. The canvas roof had a big right-angled rip and a mudguard was missing. His waistcoat hung loose and the gold watch chain was gone. He took the suitcase, gave her the familiar scratchy father's kiss on the cheek. Didn't meet her eye.

Frank had written to her: *Dad's lost the Cally.* She wanted to break the silence in the car, say, It's all right, Dad, I know. Bert was looking straight ahead, gripping the big steering wheel tight. Theirs was the only car on the street. Down by the river there was a camp of unemployed, a muddle of humpies made of sacks and flattened kerosene tins. There was a queue of men alongside the wall outside the Catholic church, heads bowed in the sun, each one with a bowl or mug in his hand waiting to be filled. A few looked up as they drove past. Their faces were blank.

Dolly came out as soon as she heard the car. Got to be out by Monday, she said by way of greeting. Nance had a moment to think, Whether it's because of something big or something small, Mum's anger sounds the same. Then she realised what her mother meant. The Cally was the nearest place to a home Nance had. Now it was finished. Not some time in the future, but next Monday.

He won't hear the word, Dolly said. Bankrupt. She said it again, loudly. Bankrupt!

They'd managed to get a farm down south in Mittagong. It wasn't much of a farm or they couldn't have got it, but Bert had wangled something.

Oh, the fool of a man, Dolly said. Her thin face was screwed tight. I told him, Turn the place into a boarding house, at least there'll be something coming in. But oh no, Mr High-and-Mighty couldn't come at that. Always going to come good tomorrow. Now here we are, Lily Maunder offering me her old dresses! Alan Russell coming along wanting to give us a hundred pound! Never been so ashamed in my life.

She was sewing up furniture in hessian to be sent down on the train to the Mittagong place. A big cedar sideboard, two chests of drawers, some chairs. Max was tying up bundles of spoons and knives engraved with *Caledonian* and slipping them into the drawers. They weren't supposed to be taking anything. Every chair and spoon in the Cally belonged to the bank now. But, with so many foreclosures, the bank was too busy to be checking on spoons.

On Monday they set off in the Fiat. Nance sat in the front next to Frank, the tall silent brother she hardly knew after so long apart. His face was expressionless. He was a man of twenty-two. Some scrubby little place at Mittagong wasn't what he'd hoped for, but it was better than being the poor relation at Uncle Willie's. Max sat in the back with Dolly, crammed in with a suitcase and bundles of clothes. He'd had to leave his bicycle and his dumb-bells and his pile of *Boy's Own* annuals. He had the sport trophies he'd won at school, but only because he'd agreed to have them on his lap all the way to Mittagong. He was eighteen now and the cuffs of his old school blazer were halfway to his elbows.

Dolly sat like a piece of metal, holding her shame hard and cold. Everyone knew the car. *Oh, there go the Russells. Bankrupt, you know.* Bert stood at the door watching. His face was set in deep grooves. He was going to settle everything up and come down on the train in a week. Nance waved but he didn't wave back.

Once they got to Mittagong she'd look for a job. Something would surely turn up for a registered pharmacist. In the crisis of the move no one had even asked to see the certificate. It hadn't seemed the right moment to say anything about being second in the state.

She watched the paddocks of Goonoo Goonoo passing, sheep scrambling away from the car. She had to pretend to be long-faced like everyone else. Inside she was telling it over to herself like counting out coins: *Never again, never again.* Never again those hated four walls, the screech of the trams, the smell of cabbage and potato on the stairs at the hostel. Rabbits weren't so bad. They could get a milking cow and they could kill a sheep now and then. They wouldn't go hungry the way those poor wretches outside the church were hungry. And, for the first time in years, they'd all be together.

When they got to Currabubula they didn't stop. The school was the same, only the pepper trees were bigger and the privies had been painted. Past the Davis Hotel with the creek at the back where she'd found her best chainies. For a moment she thought to ask Frank to pull over so she could go and see if they were still under the rock. But it was comforting to think of them always there, watching the days and nights, the heat and cold, the turning of the seasons.

Then down through Quirindi. Over the river at Murrurundi, through Scone, the paddocks full of shaggy horses that had been polo champions. Someone had told her that once you put a polo pony out to grass, it would never be any good for polo again.

They were going to spend the night at Singleton. But as they came into the town there was a police car at the side of the road, and a man flagging them down. When they stopped Nance could hear him crunching towards them along the dirt. He bent to the window. The Russells, is it? he asked. No one said anything, sitting stiffly with the certainty of disaster. Bert alone amid his ruined dream.

Message for Nance, the man said. Which one's Nance? Like a child in a classroom she put her hand up, and he gave her a piece of paper. Need to call that number, love, he said. Soon's ever you can.

She knew the number as well as she knew her own birthday. The Enmore Pharmacy. She rang from a public phone near Singleton station. Charlie Gledhill's voice sounded distant and hollow. She'd never spoken to him on the phone before. Bennetts is leaving, he said. You were my first thought, Miss Russell. Say you'll do it.

When she told them, Max grinned all over his freckled boy's face. You beauty, Nance! Frank turned to her smiling, pressing her hand, and even Dolly said, Well, thank God for that. Nance smiled and pretended. Wonderful!

All the way through dinner at the Criterion she had to keep it up. Next morning she stood at the station with the same little suitcase she'd brought to Tamworth. For three days she'd been part of a family again. She watched the Fiat turn out of the yard, saw Max waving a last cheery goodbye.

Finally she could stop smiling.

The first time around, the Enmore Pharmacy was a prison term. The second time it felt like a life sentence, with no days to mark off on the wall. At least now she was paid a wage, not an apprentice's pocket money. A registered pharmacist got five pounds a week. That was good money compared to what most people were getting in 1933. But it had to stretch a long way. After she'd paid her board and sent the family some money, and put some in the bank for just-in-case, she was left with about a pound for everything else, and there was always something. Get your shoes mended, have your hair cut, buy soap and tooth powder. Even wholesale from the shop those things cost money. New clothes were out of reach. You'd get down in the mouth if you started to think about them. The best you could do was get something from the second-hand shop and hope you could wash the musty smell out of it.

The price for that good money was that she could never leave the shop. The apprentice—she had her own now—got out occasionally to deliver an order or take the tram to Pattinson's for another bottle of Pot. Bromide. The registered pharmacist couldn't step out, not even for a moment. The longing to be able to walk out into the air became a hunger. To be out from those four walls pressing in! She didn't complain, but one day Charlie Gledhill said he'd give her Wednesday afternoon off. He'd come in for those few hours, keep his hand in. She liked him for that.

He called in at the shop most evenings on his way home from the hospital. He'd go through the books with her, decide what to order, discuss whether they should sell Bell's Vigour Pills. Nance would boil up some water on the Bunsen and they'd have a cup of tea.

She was right that he'd come from nothing much. His father was a house painter in Lithgow and without the free public schools he'd have ended up painting houses too, he said. Luckily, from Lithgow Public he'd got a place at Fort Street Boys', the best government high school in the state. Had to board with an uncle in Homebush to go there. Nance had been sent away at eight, he'd been twelve. Reckon it's why we're tough buggers, he said. You and me both.

He'd always wanted to be a surgeon, he said. Pharmacy was only ever a step on the path that could take a poor boy upwards. He'd done his apprenticeship at Five Dock Pharmacy, that was where he'd met Win. Then he'd been a demonstrator in the Pharmacy Department at the university. When they did the dates, it turned out that if he'd stayed there a year longer he would have been the one teaching Nance how to calibrate a pipette. Funny old world, isn't it, Nance, he said.

Win's father ran a nursery in Five Dock and he and his wife had taken to Charlie like the son they didn't have. They'd lent him the money to buy the business. They came to the shop with him one day and she watched Charlie showing Mr Betts everything, the different sizes of mortars and how the pill machine worked. He jollied Mrs Betts along, putting his arm around her, telling her she looked nice, launching into one of his long stories to make her smile.

At the end of the day, Nance would have the accounts book out ready for Charlie on the counter, waiting for him to swing in, bringing the life of the world into the claustrophobic shop. They'd bend over the big greasy ledger together, his finger running down the columns, Nance beside him holding the page flat.

She was Miss Russell at the start. Somewhere along the line she became Nance.

In August that year Nance turned twenty-one. Dolly and Bert sent her a watch, a dainty little thing, engraved on the back: *To Nance on her twenty-first birthday, from her parents.* It was a normal present for a twenty-first and useful for getting to the shop on time. Nance knew they couldn't guess what a nightmare of clock-watching her life was. When she pressed the little latch into place around her wrist it was like locking herself to that life forever.

Bert's letters were always full of how things would soon look up, but Nance didn't see any sign of it. It had been four years now since the Depression had started. The churches couldn't cope any more with so many hungry people, women and little children as well as men lining up for a bowl of soup. It was so bad now that, if you could prove you were starving, the government would give you food orders that you could take to the grocery and get a few basic things. Mothers came into the pharmacy with government orders for baby food.

Some pharmacies would only sell a shilling's worth of anything that had to be dispensed. By the time you mixed up whatever it was, it wasn't worth doing it for less than that. Charlie said, We'll make sixpennorth our lowest price. But a lot of people only had the threepence and Nance couldn't send them away. If someone was sick you had to help them.

The worst of it was the skinny people coming around trying to sell things: brooms, feather dusters, shoelaces, boxes of matches. Ten or fifteen in a day. You'd buy something from one, but then there'd be another. You couldn't buy something from all of them, but how could you turn them away?

It sounded miserable at the Mittagong farm, too, looking after sheep that no one wanted to buy, putting in crops that didn't fetch what it cost to harvest them, rabbits the only thing there was plenty of. Still, the Russells were among the lucky ones.

Frank was too old to be living with Mum and Dad and his little brother, and too clever to spend his best years skinning rabbits for a bob a pelt. He wrote to Nance about land being balloted, Crown leases that had been turned back to the government. *Could you lend me fifty pounds?* he wrote. *You have to put that up to go in the ballot, show you're serious.* If he didn't get the land he'd get the money back, and if he did get it he promised he'd pay her back as quick as quick. Fifty pounds was about all she had in the bank. It was frightening, seeing the teller write what was left: two pounds ten and fourpence.

Frank won a block in Queensland, a place called Bringalily, west of Brisbane. The lease had been surrendered because the land had been covered with prickly pear, but now the government had got some sort of caterpillar that ate the stuff and the place was mostly clear, Frank said. He was going to live in a tent and go to work on the roads until he had enough to get a cottage up and buy a few milkers.

Nance wrote to say she wanted to go with him, would do anything to get out of the pharmacy, had no fear of living in a tent. Compared with the pharmacy that kind of hardship sounded like paradise. But Frank said no. *Not that I wouldn't like your company, Nance,* he wrote. *My worry is, it'll be rough at the start. If it's me on my own I can manage, but I'd be anxious about you.*

When she got the letter she cried and cried. Hadn't known till she started to cry how she'd longed to be with Frank, working side by side, brother and sister again. Even after she wanted to stop crying she couldn't. Some machine in her had been started up and she had no power to turn it off. Matron had to be called, hold the sal volatile under her nose. Afterwards she thought she might never feel anything, ever again.

Meg Naughton was still teaching at Lawson. She'd met a man there, a German, and they'd have got married but Meg wanted to keep her job, so they were living, as Meg wrote, in sin. It was a risk, she'd be sacked on the spot if anyone found out. How unfair, she said. Why should my brains wither on the vine for the sole reason that I'm a woman?

Nance missed her but with no money for the train they couldn't see each other often. There were some new women at the hostel who Nance got to be friends with. Molly worked in a shop. Every morning she put fresh newspaper in her shoes where the soles were gone. It was lucky she was behind the counter all day, she said, so no one saw. Rete was a qualified accountant but no one needed accountants so she had a job as a filing clerk. Considered herself lucky to get three pounds ten a week. Her dream was to have a bookshop. She'd talk about it over dinner as if it really existed. How she'd arrange the stock, what she'd put in the window. Nance tried to think of her own dream, but there was a blank where a dream might have been. She hadn't found it before the pharmacy years, and those years had stifled everything else.

When you were on your own there were a lot of rules you didn't have to take any notice of. One of them was that a respectable young woman should live in a church hostel. Molly and Rete and Nance found a boarding house nearby that would cost the same, but without the rules. They slept in the one room, Molly and Rete in the double bed and Nance in a stretcher in the corner. It was like having sisters, plenty of fun and no secrets. At bedtime Rete put sticky stuff on her hands and then gloves, because of her dry skin. On a Friday night Molly put her hair in papers so she'd look nice for her afternoon off. They told Nance that castor oil made eyelashes grow, so Nance smeared it on every night. No matter how bad things were, you had to believe that one day you'd be living in a world where it mattered if you had soft hands and long eyelashes.

At night everyone gathered in the parlour to play cards. Nance was always late getting in because of the shop, but the others would wait for her. It was something to look forward to, walking into a room full of people pleased to see you.

Oc was a good bridge partner, and he was sweet on her, but she wasn't interested. And what was his mother thinking, calling him Octavius, even if he was the eighth child? The one she liked was Don McDonald. He was Canadian, had come for a visit and more or less got stuck when the Depression hit. Couldn't play cards to save his life but was musical. He had a job at Paling's in the city, demonstrating the pianos, and he could belt out anything on Mrs Cahill's old upright.

Oh, give us 'Smoke Gets in Your Eyes', Oc would call out. He'd watch Nance while Don sang, but she'd be watching Don. He'd be singing in his light tuneful voice, smiling at her through the words about the bright flame of love, and she'd be smiling back. She felt bad for poor Oc, but you didn't have any control over who you were drawn to. Still, Don would be going back to Canada, he made no secret of that. There was no future in it.

It was a funny home-made social world at the boarding house, the girls all crammed together two or three to a room, the boys down the hall in theirs, everyone playing cards and eyeing each other. But what could you do other than flirt across the table? The men weren't in any position to get married. If they had jobs at all, they were poor sorts of jobs. Nance thought of all those young men and women, all over Sydney, all over Australia, all over the world, their bright days melting away. No chance to pair off when nature intended them to, and when would that chance come? For a woman, the time of being desirable was so short.

Oh, this is a terrible life, she said. Our lives are passing!

She'd never lived before with people who talked about politics but at the boarding house everyone knew what should be done. Mr Bannerman, an older man who went door to door with doilies, was sure that things would come right if you left them alone. It wasn't the government's job to look after people, he said. The invisible hand of the market—supply and demand—was the only way for things to come right. Oc and Don disagreed. With no one spending any money, how was demand ever going to get supply going again unless the government got money back into circulation? They got vehement about it, because it wasn't an abstraction, it was their lives. Some nights Mrs Cahill had to come in and read the riot act.

Nance had never heard of deflation, didn't know who Keynes was, or how to argue about the invisible hand. But she thought about how it had been at the Cally. As soon as the guests stopped coming, Dolly and Bert had to let all the staff go. Without jobs, those people had stopped spending. That meant all the little shops that had relied on them went bust. Then the shop people in turn stopped spending. It was as inevitable as gravity. Unless the government stepped in and broke that cycle there was no reason anything would ever change. Nance had always thought about what was happening around her as an act of nature, like the weather. She began to see that events occurred because men in London and

Washington and Canberra made one decision rather than another.

Now she was over twenty-one she could enrol to vote. There was an election coming up in 1934 and she went down to the local school with the others on voting day. As she marked the boxes she could hear Mr Bannerman's scorn. He'd never quite said so, but she had a feeling Mr Bannerman didn't think ignorant people like her should be allowed to vote.

The conservatives won again, but not by much. Labor got one million, five hundred and fifty-five thousand, seven hundred and thirty-seven votes. She looked at that last digit and thought, That's my vote. My voice.

SIX

AT THE start of 1937 Charlie graduated with honours and two prizes for surgery, and started his residency at the hospital. One night at the shop he said he had a favour to ask. As a resident he often had to spend the night at the hospital and Win didn't like being alone in the flat. Would Nance go and stay with her now and then? It was an easy favour to grant. She liked Win and it made a change from the boarding house. Win would make tea for them, she was a good cook, then they'd have a few hands of rummy and Win would tell the story of falling in love with Charlie, how she went into the Five Dock Pharmacy one day for cough syrup and there he was.

Charlie and Win had planned to wait until he got through Medicine before they started a family, and a few months into his residency Win was starting to show. But every time Nance went to the flat, Win was less well.

Nausea, palpitations, swollen ankles. Win made light of it. Oh, Charlie doesn't seem worried and he's the doctor! In the shop, though, Charlie was more and more preoccupied. One night it all spilled out. Win had eclampsia: high blood pressure. She was taking magnesium sulphate and avoiding excitement but that was only a half measure, not a cure. The only cure was to get the baby out. The problem was, Win wasn't far enough along. The baby would die if delivered now. She might die, too, from the shock. But if you waited until the baby was sure to survive, the mother could go into convulsions and they could both die. On a great shuddering sigh Charlie said, It puts the doctor in a terrible position, Nance. There was a silence between them because it wasn't just *the doctor*, any stranger. The doctor was the husband and the father, and he was haggard with the choice that had to be made.

A few weeks later Nance had hardly opened up the shop when the call came through. Charlie's voice was strangled, a thickness around every word. She'd never heard a man cry before. Win had gone into convulsions. They'd done an emergency Caesarean but it was too late. Mother and baby were both dead. Nance said, Oh, how terrible, I'm so sorry, and there was a long silence. She squeezed the receiver hard, pressed her ear to it. Finally she heard the click of him hanging up.

Win's father phoned later. Could you close the shop, please, Miss Russell? His voice was brisk and businesslike. She understood that Mr Betts was one of those men who needed to be busy and not stop to think. She inked a black edge around a sheet of paper, wrote the phrases she'd seen on other shop doors.

At the funeral Charlie's face was warped by grief. She lined up with everyone else and spoke to him. He glanced at her without seeing, pressed her hand. She was nothing but another person who wasn't his dead wife. She saw his white lips say, Thank you, thank you. Then she had to let the next person take his cold hand and murmur something that he didn't hear, and have him say, Thank you, thank you.

It was Nance's first death. While the clergyman talked about someone called Winice, she thought about Win, the fun they'd had. Everything they'd done seemed significant. For a lark she and Win had read each other's palms one night. She remembered the silkiness of Win's skin, the warmth of her fingers, the weight of her hand. The lines on the palm were neat, like embroidery, the flesh rosy. Now that hand was in the coffin. It would be cold and pale, stiff by now. No one would ever hold it again. No one would ever sit with Win over a bottle of beer and laugh themselves to tears about the silly things in the palm-reading book. That was what death was. Nothing solemn or grand, just a hole in the world. She looked at her own hand. It would be in a coffin, cold and dark, one day. Then it would just be the bones she could see under the skin.

Afterwards Mr Betts came up to her. Keep the shop closed, Miss Russell, he said. A month. Let's say six weeks.

Mr Gledhill told me to tell you specially, thank you for your support and naturally you'll be paid. He glanced at her for the first time and she saw how his eyes were shrunken in their sockets, the blue of them bright against the bloodshot whites.

For once it was Nance waiting for the others at the boarding house that night. They said to shut the shop, she told them. What will you do, Nance? they wanted to know. She opened her mouth to say, I don't know, and found that she'd said, I'll go and see the family.

She knew then that she'd never leave behind the longing. *Family.* She'd thought that seven years of pharmacy had driven it into the ground. But the less a family was a family, the more the longing for it would never leave. She thought, On my deathbed I'll still be longing.

The place Frank had won at Bringalily had been covered with the wreckage of prickly pear when he'd gone there. No stock, no crops, no house. He'd worked a long time on the roads around Bringalily to get a bit of cash. *Reckon I'm the champion gravel-spreader of Queensland*, he wrote. Once the farm was up and running, Dolly and Max had joined him. Bert stayed on at Mittagong. No one spelled it out, but it was a way of quietly burying a dead marriage.

Nance went to Mittagong first. The farm was a dry stony place, always windy, the little house creaking. None of that mattered. Not being locked up in the pharmacy was a delight she didn't tire of. It was enough to get up in the morning and live the day through, walking out into the yard or up on the gaunt paddocks whenever she pleased. She thought, The wonderful thing about hard times is that you don't need a Caribbean cruise. It's enough to have the day to yourself.

Whether it was the shame of the bankruptcy that could never be mentioned, or not having to deal with Dolly, she didn't know, but her father was a good companion in the evenings by the fire, gentler and quieter than she remembered. For the first time he was willing to talk about personal things.

Your mother never thought I was good enough for her, he said. Mind you, she might have been right. On her good days you had to go to the front parlour to get someone better than your mother.

He laughed, rubbed his hands up and down his thighs the way he did when he was thinking about something.

Remember Rothsay, Nance, he said. Never any good there. My word, the rows we had! She threw me out once, you know. Frank a little baby. Then she changed her mind, sent word, would I come back. Well, I did in the end and you were the result. You were a fluke, Nance.

The window made its little song in the night wind, a shingle rattled up on the roof. He stared peacefully into the fire, rubbing the nap of his trousers as if he'd said nothing of importance. A fluke! She'd always known she wasn't wanted. Otherwise why would her parents have sent her away so much? She'd thought nothing could be more bleak than knowing. She was wrong. Here it was, something worse: being told.

Bert got up to pour himself another whisky but stopped behind her chair and ruffled her hair, the way he'd done when she was little. Good having you here, Nance, he said. She knew what he was saying, and knew he'd never be able to say it. She touched his hand, held it for a moment. You had to take what you were offered.

The village near Frank's place was called Bringalily on the sign, but Frank told Nance that it should really be spelled Bringalilli, because it didn't have anything to do with bringing lilies. It was the name of the Aboriginal tribe of the area and should be pronounced with a hard 'g'. He'd got to be mates with a man who'd worked on the roads with him, he said. Half Aboriginal, had told him a few things about the old ways. Seems only right to say it their way, Frank said. Least we can do, all things considered.

It was a Frank she'd never known before, someone who thought about such things as the right way to say an Aboriginal word. She'd never thought about anything like that herself, though once he told her she made a point of saying it the Aboriginal way. It made her realise how little she knew Frank, how far apart they'd grown since those sweet years at Rothsay. It was hard when you'd been separated for so long. A letter was no good for the small things like that, the ones that told you who the other person really was. For those things you had to be there day by day.

Dolly was calmer and more cheerful at Bringalily than Nance had ever seen her. She'd thrown herself into helping Frank. He'd dug a dairy, three-quarters underground, and she'd rigged up a clever system of hessian curtains and water troughs to make it cool, so they'd get the top grade, choicest, from the butter people. She was full of all her other plans to make things better. Nance watched her pour water into the troughs that kept the hessian wet. Oh, Mum, she thought. You should have been a man, or born later.

The place was doing pretty well, but even easygoing Max was sick of the cows. You had to milk them at dawn and dusk, no matter what. Frank had gone in another ballot, for some land at Guyra, not far from Tamworth. Sheep and potato country, he said. You can have a sleep in now and then.

He'd got to know the neighbours, all dairy farmers. Their lives revolved around the milking. They'd come over in the evenings, though everyone went to bed early. Being the host was a side of Frank she'd never seen. He was warm and smiling, quietly making sure everyone had what they wanted and heading off Dolly if she started to get hot under the collar.

And Frank, have you got anyone? she asked him one morning, walking back from the milking. She glanced up in time to catch a grimace.

Yes, he said. Norah. She lives along the way. You'd like her, Nance.

Well, she said. Well, Frank? Smiling up at him, but Frank didn't look at her.

Norah, well, he said. She's Norah Gallagher. Catholics. You know what Mum's like about Catholics.

It never made sense, Frank, she said. Wouldn't have a bar of Catholics but sent me off to the nuns.

You don't look to Mum to make sense, he said. All I know is, she won't have Norah in the house.

Nance could see it: the family divided all over again, *Never darken my door!* That iron will of Dolly's. Nance wanted to say, Go ahead anyway, Frank, it'll work out if you love Norah and she loves you. But what if she was wrong, what if the Catholic thing meant more misery for everyone?

When Nance got back home to Sydney, Frank wrote to her. He and Dolly had had a row about Norah, Frank called it the Row to End All Rows. *Mum promised she'd make our lives hell*, he wrote. *But I should have stuck to my guns for once.*

He'd won the land at Guyra, a place called Green Hills, but Dolly didn't want to leave Bringalily. *Well enough where we are*, she grumbled to Nance in her letters, *I don't know why Frank's got to be always on the move.* Nance laughed so loudly she startled the others in the dining room.

She thought the real trouble with Guyra was that it was too close to Tamworth. Too much shame there. And too close to Currabubula. Dolly had grown up on a farm scratching out a living, and at Guyra she'd be doing it again.

Bert was leaving Mittagong and going to Guyra. He knew about sheep. Max went along with things in his easygoing way. Milk a cow, crutch a sheep. It was all the same to him.

SEVEN

THE SECOND night the shop in Enmore was open again, Charlie came in. He had on his big black overcoat, the September nights were still cold and thin rain was making the street gleam. Nance was awkward behind the counter, trying to think of words that would bridge the chasm between someone who'd never known the death of a loved person and someone who'd been crushed by it.

He lifted the counter-flap, came around to the narrow space behind. She'd got the ledger out open, it was there on the counter in front of them. He looked at it and she thought he was reading the day's numbers. Then he turned to her and put his arms around her, the big coat lapping them in its folds. They stood for a long time. She breathed in his smell, maleness and damp wool, a hint of the hospital he'd come from. She felt his chest rising and falling against her. She hoped he wasn't crying. He put his hands on her shoulders, pushed a little distance between them, kissed her on the forehead, a brotherly sort of moment. Thank you, Nance, he said. Thanks.

The next night when he came he had fish and chips for them in steamy paper parcels. They stood at the counter together putting chips into their mouths, breaking off bits of yellow batter and flakes of fish. He pointed at 7/6 in a column and left a greasy translucent shape on the page, wiped at it with his handkerchief, spread the stain into the next column. Out, out, damned spot, he said.

Yet who would have thought the old man to have had so much blood in him, she said, and as she said it she worried, Should I be talking about blood, will it remind him? She wanted to mention Win, though, make her normal again, and he must have been thinking along the same lines because he said, You know, Win never did the Leaving, didn't know any Shakespeare. Regarded me as some kind of genius. Didn't realise we'd all learned yards of it.

She admired you, Nance said. Told me you were the cleverest, handsomest man she'd ever met.

She remembered the slippery feel of the cards, the yellow light in Win's kitchen, Win half laughing at herself but in earnest too.

I was a lucky man, Charlie said. And then we ran out of luck.

Win was with them from then on, a comfortable memory. She couldn't imagine you'd ever get over a death like that. You wouldn't want to pretend it hadn't happened, or that it didn't matter. Still, you wouldn't want to live every minute in its shadow.

One Saturday he asked her to the dog races at Harold Park. Said he knew a man who owned one of the dogs, that was why he wanted to go. But they never saw the man and Charlie didn't seem interested in one dog more than the others. They went to the pictures a few times. No romances, only comedies. They'd come out into the late afternoon and he'd stride along the footpath not looking back. He was abrupt, spoke to her like a man talking to himself, not waiting for an answer. A picnic at the Audley Weir, the bush ticking all around, sandstone glowing golden where the sun hit it, old men fishing along the wall. He hired one of the boats and rowed her along but, although their legs were touching, he didn't look at her. There seemed no way to have a conversation with a man whose eyes were always elsewhere, even when he was rowing you along a picturesque stretch of the Audley River, and who kissed you in that brotherly way at the end of each excursion.

He took it for granted that she was experienced. He knew about the men at the boarding house, how they waited for her to come back from the shop. Called them her admirers. She didn't know how to tell him that they weren't, or if they were it was all one way. He was a man broken apart by what he'd seen, what he'd heard, the dead child he'd held, the choice he'd made, and the question that never left him. What if he'd done things differently?

He flailed around, she could see that, anything to stop the boiling away of those memories.

He'd only be in Sydney for another couple of months. He had a place at Edinburgh, he'd do his surgical training there. He'd booked his berth on the boat and put the business on the market. Now and then men would turn up and go through the ledger with him, stamp on the floorboards, turn the taps on and off.

One night he came to the shop with a glitter about him. He'd been drinking, she could smell it. But he was steady enough. He came up to her at the counter like a customer, closed the ledger, took her hands. Come on out of there, he said, and smiled a version of the old charmer's smile.

He drove them to the little road beside the Lane Cove River, the winding dirt track pale in the starlight. Stopped the car under shifting black trees and everything was suddenly silent. They call this Lovers' Lane, he said. Where we are, here. She heard the thinness in his voice, he wasn't quite sure any more. But she was. Shifted on the creaking leather seat, a fraction towards him, and that was enough, he was on her like a starving man.

She was willing, more than willing. Oh, it was wonderful to be there in the dark with him, the water rustling across the stones. He'd brought a blanket for them to lie on and it was a warm night. She saw the stars through the trees, and the cut-out shape of a fruit bat gliding over the river. The water glimmered, a fish jumped. He pushed her back onto the blanket, she heard the buckle of his belt and the ripping of the package of the french letter.

Nance thought he'd be sorry afterwards, was braced for him to be cool to her in the shop, turn the ledger round so he wouldn't have to come in behind the counter beside her. But they went back to Lane Cove. She got to know the shape of the trees above them, though the stars and moon were in a different place every night. After that first painful time, it was a pleasure that was always a surprise. He was a tender lover and could see the funny side of it, always had a joke to ease the awkward business of getting the french letter on.

She loved him, of course. Had loved him for ages, back when he sat next to her in the dark at the Enmore Cinema. Clever and witty but with a heart and, although he was a doctor now, they were from the same world. The Lithgow back streets of his childhood weren't so different from the working men's pubs of her own. Her father had struck lucky and made money and his hadn't, but neither she nor Charlie was born with the silver spoon.

She loved him, but she wasn't going to fall in love, because what was the point? He needed a woman, needed comfort and company, and he liked her well enough. She'd be a fool to think there was any more to it than that. So when he said, Nance, why don't you come with me to Edinburgh, she was surprised, but dismissed it as the impulse of a warm moment. The next night he said it again. Come with me, Nance. Why not? Shout you your ticket.

This time she thought about it. Edinburgh. She'd find work, pharmacy was the same wherever you were. But she tried to imagine their lives. He'd be the promising young surgeon. She'd be Miss Russell, his half-educated pharmacist friend from the colonies.

And he was saying, Come with me. He wasn't saying, Marry me. Not that she cared about marriage in itself, but *Marry me* would mean he liked her for more than a bit of comfort after his wife had died. *Marry me* meant *I love you*. He wasn't saying that.

She went down to the wharf to see him off. Had to fight herself at the last touch not to say, I'll get on the next boat! She stood beside his father, come down from Lithgow. He was a rough sort of a man from somewhere in England and spoke with such a strong accent she had to keep asking him to repeat himself. She hadn't known his father was English. He was happy to see his son returning in triumph to the place he'd left as a hungry immigrant.

She held the streamer, looked up at the face that was already made small and anonymous by distance. When the streamer stretched and broke and the ship swivelled and Charlie was lost to sight, his father turned to her. Ah well, he said. Now there's a good man. His eyelashes were stuck together with his tears.

Charlie had fixed up a job for her at the hospital where he'd trained. Be a walk in the park, he said. None of the damn customers. But at Prince Alfred it was Mr Denning with his steel-rimmed glasses, never speaking except to tell

Nance to use a smaller bottle, or rouse on her for gluing the label on crooked, and what's this doing here? Nance was surprised that she missed the customers. You never knew if they'd be kind or rude, whether they'd wheedle for credit or flirt, and that kept the day interesting. In the high-ceilinged silent austerity of the hospital dispensary, she even began to long for the noise of the trams.

She met a pharmacist from Prince Henry Hospital, the Coast Hospital, near Maroubra. Joan told her about a vacancy there. You'd like it, she said. We have a bit of fun. Nance applied and got an interview. The man wanted to know if she was thinking of getting married. No, she said, and she could hear the coldness in her voice, because there'd never been any talk of marriage, and now he was gone. The interviewer looked at her appraisingly. Oh, how she hated the way men looked you up and down! She knew what he was thinking: Twenty-five. What's wrong with her, why is she still on the shelf?

There were only three of them in the dispensary at the Coast, the third a pleasant man named Duncan who she came to realise went home at night to his boyfriend. Joan was a Catholic and was supposed to disapprove, but as long as Duncan was discreet she could pretend she didn't know. There was something about him that reminded her of Arthur at the Cally, and gradually she realised that Arthur and Con must have been a couple like Duncan and his friend. She watched Duncan holding up a bottle to pour something, his face intent, a man like any other, except that he could go to jail for whatever it was that he and his friend did at night. Being a woman in a man's world wasn't easy, but you didn't go to jail for it.

They worked hard, but only from nine to five. They had every third Saturday off, and no work on Sundays. For the first time in nearly eight years she had a weekend, even if it was only once a month.

The Coast Hospital was out of town, a hundred acres looking out to sea. It had started in the nineteenth century as a place for people with smallpox. When Nance went there smallpox was in the past but there was a lock hospital on the grounds for the people with syphilis and a lazaret for the lepers. The main hospital dealt with diphtheria, typhoid, tuberculosis, all the worst contagious things. You didn't go to the Coast if your leg was broken.

That might have been why it had a particular feel to it. Not a hospital of crisis so much as a hospital of lost lives, men and women shut away with only each other and the nurses and doctors for society. The lepers were mostly Chinese. They had a vegetable garden and she could see them from the window of the dispensary, walking backwards and forwards in their big conical hats with drums of water on sticks across their shoulders. When the weather was good they'd bring their mahjong outside and on a still day you could hear the click and clatter of the tiles.

The nurses had made a rock pool where they swam in summer, had a raft that they poled around the bay.

They lived with death every day. Now and then one of them caught something from a patient and died. Just the same, at lunchtime they all went down to the little beach and swam in the home-made rock pool as carefree as if they'd never heard of dying.

She thought about Charlie. Every day at first, then less often. You had to look forward. That was something she'd learned. If you looked back at the good times you'd only make yourself miserable. Life wasn't going to hand anything to you. You had to go out and find it.

Charlie wrote to her from Aden and again from the boarding house in Edinburgh. She wrote back and he wrote again. Every time a letter arrived, so did the wondering. His letters always began *My dear Nance*. She thought, Perhaps he liked me more than I realised. But he never wrote, *I'm in love with you. Come to Edinburgh and we'll get married.* His letters began to feel like a taunt. The wittier they were, the warmer and more affectionate, the worse they made her feel. *Look, here's what you're not going to have.*

She turned twenty-six in August 1938. Joan made a cake and Duncan brought candles. At lunchtime they went down to the beach with some of the nurses. The candles kept blowing out in the breeze and the singing was thin out in the open air. *Happy birthday, dear Na-ance.* A few of the lepers came down to the top of the ridge and when it came to *Hip-hip, hooray* they cheered too.

She stood with the slice of cake in her hand looking out to the sea that had taken Charlie away. The waves came in, sucked out, came in again. He was gone. She thought, If I've made a mistake not going with him, I've made it. Best stop thinking about him.

She moved to a boarding house in Maroubra to be closer to the hospital. By chance Wade Watson from the old days at Tamworth High was living there. He had a job doing something with the machines at the *Sydney Morning Herald*. He was sweet on Joan and came out to the hospital once a week pretending to teach her German. But he was Presbyterian, so Joan couldn't let herself be interested in him, and anyway there was a Harry Mulhall she was keen on. Nance wasn't interested in Wade either, not in that way, but her life seemed to be a pattern of making friends and then being separated from them. Being with someone who'd known her at school made her feel connected to the world in the way other people were.

She had something like a proper social life now. She'd met Jake Killen at university and ran into him again one day in the city. He'd become a teacher. He was a thoughtful kindly man and he was definitely interested, just waiting for a signal from her. Then there was Wal Glendon. Ever since she'd been in Sydney she'd seen him once a week at Sunday lunch. She knew how cheerful he always was, no matter what. Knew what he looked like with his mother's apron round his waist, washing up. He'd lost his job with the trams and now he was like so many men, trying for anything that was going. He'd set out to queue for another job, the comb-marks deep in his hair, still smiling even after so many knockbacks. Now and then he got work driving a truck or loading ships' cargo, but they laid you off as soon as they didn't need you. He was a good man, she knew, and she caught a tender look from him now and then.

She wasn't in love with Jake or Wal, although she knew either of them would make a good husband. She wondered if some part of her might always belong to Charlie Gledhill. There was some old wives' tale about the first man you slept with imprinting you for the rest of your life. In that case, she thought, does it matter who I pick?

EIGHT

WHEN NANCE took the job at the Coast Hospital it was the first time anyone in her family had been employed by the government. As far back as Solomon Wiseman, it was only ever men working for themselves, thieving or farming or running pubs. At the Enmore Pharmacy she'd worked for wages, but those wages came from the profit Mr Stevens or Charlie Gledhill made. Now her pay packet came from the government, and the medicines she dispensed were given out free to the people who needed them. All of that came from tax.

If you were in business on your own account, tax was something you avoided if you could. In their palmy days Bert and Dolly were forever complaining. They'd worked for their money, why shouldn't they keep it? Now that Nance was a *servant* of the *public* she saw it differently. If no one paid tax, there'd be no Coast Hospital. There'd be no free nurses and doctors and no pharmacists giving out free medicine. There'd have been no Currabubula Public School to give her parents just enough education to leave that failed farm. No high school to give their daughter choices and opportunities.

Looked at that way, the state wasn't a thief taking people's money. It was how a community worked. Everyone made a contribution so that no one missed out. It didn't go as far as *from each according to his ability, to each according to his need,* but it was trying to make things fairer.

Meg's kind of socialism had always been too radical for Nance, but she was starting to see that socialism came in different shades. Wade Watson called himself a socialist. At the same time he believed in marriage and family and went to church, a steady Tamworth boy.

On a Sunday, Wade would get a group of them together to go down to the Domain to hear the soapbox speakers. It was a great afternoon's entertainment. There were men who shouted that the Second Coming was nigh, one wrapped in nothing but a sheet who said clothes were against nature. The famous Bea Miles would be there, a vast woman in a tennis eyeshade and an overcoat, reciting Shakespeare. Nance listened but hung back because Bea was unpredictable, could pounce on you and hold your arm while she declaimed into your face. Remember Mr Crisp, Wade? Nance would say, but Wade had never gone in much for poetry.

Wade knew a bit about the Christian Socialists. That one was a teacher, he told Nance, that one was a lawyer, and the man up on the box now was actually a church minister, though he wasn't wearing his dog collar. Nance saw what Wade was telling her: they weren't revolutionaries, any more than he was. They'd just lived through the last ten years.

Living through them had changed her, too. Her parents had been on their own doing the best they could for themselves, but there was another way, where people looked out for each other. It was better, she was coming to think, to live in a world where things were shared around so everyone had enough.

One Sunday in September 1939 they all gathered around the wireless in the parlour. Menzies was going to come on and make an announcement. Everyone knew what he was going to say but you had to hear it with your own ears. *Fellow Australians, it is my melancholy duty to inform you officially that, in consequence of a persistence by Germany in her invasion of Poland, Great Britain has declared war upon her and that, as a result, Australia is also at war.*

Nance had seen the little man with the moustache on the newsreels, standing at his stone pulpit, his arm pumping up and down, haranguing great crowds that seemed like machines, line after line of people in the same uniforms thrusting their arms in the air. But it was on the other side of the world and in another language. It was serious but not personal. It was Britain's war. The man with the moustache was frightening but he was also a bit ridiculous.

Max enlisted straight away. He was twenty-four

years old. He sent Nance the photo he'd had taken in his uniform, Sergeant Walter Maxwell Russell, serious and proud, going off to join what Menzies called *the great family of nations*. A sister's eye could see it wasn't really about any of that. Being a soldier promised more fun than digging potatoes on Frank's farm. By Christmas, Max had sailed away to Europe. Everyone agreed it would all be over in a few months.

New Year's Eve, 1939. Wal and Nance were in the middle of a mass of shouting, singing, dancing people outside the GPO in Martin Place where the big clock on the tower would mark midnight. They'd had a few drinks and now Nance wished she hadn't, it was horrible and claustrophobic being packed tight in the crush. There was a frantic feeling, everyone on edge, as if they were waiting for something to happen. No one knew what 1940 was going to bring.

Near Wal and Nance some young men were looking for trouble. One jumped on the top of a tram and pulled the trolley pole off the overhead wires, so that blue sparks showered over everyone. Nance screamed, but Wal put himself between her and the sparks, wrapping his arms around her. He pulled her through the crowd till they could see the clock, and they roared along with everyone else, counting down the seconds till the big solemn hand swung up. Nineteen thirty-nine was over. Nance could see Wal's mouth shaping the words of 'Auld Lang Syne' but all she could hear were the whistles, the trumpets and rattles, the hooting of the ferries and the ships down in the harbour, one great swell of noise.

What was the point of resisting when Wal pulled her close and kissed her, when his hand slid down into the neckline of her dress? She kissed him back, two bodies together, only their clothes keeping them apart.

He didn't precisely say, Will you marry me, and she didn't exactly say, Yes, I will. But it seemed that they had what people called an understanding. Next day she thought about it and wasn't sorry. She liked him more than any other man she knew. And she could keep them both, if he wasn't too proud. It wasn't modest to think it, but she knew she had brains enough for both of them.

No one knew how much time they had. After a quiet start, the war was going badly. Most of Europe was in German hands. Now only France stood between Germany and England. Max had thought he'd be fighting in Europe but the war was in North Africa too, and he was there somewhere. Libya was the last they'd heard. The casualty lists were longer every week. Life was suddenly very short. There was a feeling of grasping what you could.

One steamy day in January she got home to the boarding house to find Wade on the doorstep waiting for her. Don't take your coat off, he said. Bishop Moyes is on at the Trades Hall, we'll make it if we hurry. She'd never heard of Bishop Moyes but Wade had a hand under her elbow, talking as he hustled her along to the bus. Bishop of Armidale, but a real firebrand, one of those Christian Socialists. You'll like it, Nance, I promise.

They slipped into the last empty seats. Nance's lap was full of handbag and scarf and she dropped her umbrella. The man next to her picked it up and handed it back. Somehow it slipped again and he picked it up but gestured that he'd hang on to it this time.

She was disappointed when Moyes came onto the platform. He had pointed ears like a pixie and leaned to one side as if not sure he was in the right place. But when he started speaking he was electrifying. Every country has its evil dream, he said. *Evil dream!* It was like poetry. The well-to-do will always resist change, he said. But society is unjust. The man next to her waved her umbrella and shouted, Bravo!

Good thing I agree, she thought, because it's my umbrella he's cheering with. She caught his eye, the thought making her smile.

She and Wade stayed for the cup of tea and sandwich afterwards. The man with her umbrella came up to her. Offered her the milk jug although she already had milk, helped her to the sugar though she didn't want any. About her own age, thin, dark, with crinkly dark hair springing back from a high forehead. After the business of the milk and the sugar, he didn't seem to know what to do to extend the moment. A lifetime of being the new girl meant that she did.

His name was Kenneth Gee. She had to get him

to say it twice. Like Moyes, he was a Christian Socialist. The Christian part was that he was a lay preacher. The socialist part was that he was secretary of the Auburn branch of the Labor Party. He was lively, witty, had a way of turning a phrase so it showed an unexpected humorous angle. Told her that he lived with his parents in a house called Banksias, but there was such a big mortgage it should be called Commercial Banksias. He kept her laughing as they stood there with their teacups tilting. He was educated and on the inside of the mysterious business of politics, living in a bigger world than she'd ever had the chance to know. She'd never met a man like him.

Wade saw which way the wind was blowing and kept away, but the tea was drunk and she knew they'd have to be getting back. She thought Ken was interested, but she got the feeling he didn't have much experience with women. She guessed at a nice middle-class background where you beat around the bush. Well, if she wasn't a bit bold she'd never see this fellow again, so she came straight out and said, What about I come and hear you preach one day? Ken didn't miss a beat. Homebush Congregational Church, he said, as if it had been his idea. Sunday, five o'clock.

Up in the pulpit in his suit he looked distinguished and even handsome in an intense dark way. He spoke for half an hour without using a single note. Eloquence, she thought. This is what eloquence is. Afterwards they had tea and a bun at the station. She'd been right about the background. He was a solicitor, worked in his father's legal practice in Auburn. It turned out he'd gone to Fort Street Boys', like Charlie Gledhill, although ten years later. He'd got first-class honours in English at the Leaving. First-class honours!

He asked her out. Not to the pictures or the beach, but to hear him give a lecture about free speech. Apparently the government was suppressing it. Being asked to go to something serious, watching him convince everyone in the audience, revealed another layer of life. With her background—only a shallow education, and parents who didn't know how to think beyond the next business opening—she'd never known it was there. Beyond her little daily round, there was a bigger world, where people looked at why things were the way they were, and worked out how to make them better. It was all new to her, but she was ready to learn.

After the lecture he sold copies of a pamphlet he'd published: *The Threat to Democracy.* Seeing his name in print was a shock. Kenneth Gee, LL.B. No one she knew had ever had their name in print, let alone with a degree after it. He gave her a copy. *For Nance, with my warmest regards, Ken.*

His next invitation was to go along with him to a meeting of the Auburn branch of the Labor Party. A bit boring, I'm afraid, he said. Boredom seems to be the opiate of the Labor Party. He laughed, and she laughed too, though she wasn't sure she got the joke. You'll have the chance to meet Lang, he said. He's president of the branch. Even Nance had heard of Jack Lang, the famous fiery ex-premier of New South Wales.

When she shook hands with Lang he looked away over her head, but it was something to shake hands with someone so famous. The meeting went on forever, with men rising to their feet with a sheaf of closely typed pages about something called a Point of Order and droning away for half an hour at a time. Terribly dull, but exciting too, to be present at what Ken called *democracy in the raw*. When she wrote to Bert he wrote back, *My word, Nance, you are moving in high circles!*

They fell into a pattern. Ken would ring up and ask her to a meeting, or down to the Domain to listen to the speakers. A few times they went to the Trocadero. He was a good dancer, light on his feet, proud of his foxtrot.

He was definitely interested. But it was a coming-and-going-away kind of liking. There were long gaps between the phone calls, and each time they met it was as if she had to start all over again. There were many times when he could have found an excuse to touch her. She made sure of that, walked close to him, her handbag on the other arm. But he never did.

She wondered if the churchy business made him prim. He might be too religious for her. One night she told him, You know, Ken, I'm not sure I believe in God. As she said it she had the image of one of those two-way gates they used to sort sheep. Ken might open the gate and let her go back out to the paddock, but it turned out he wasn't sure about God either. A church full of people was a captive audience, he said. He laughed, but she wasn't sure what sort of laugh it was. Was it because he'd fooled the kindly minister at the Homebush Congregational Church? Or was he laughing at her, for believing that he could be so cynical?

His interest was flattering and, when he turned the beam of his attention on her, he was irresistible. She was never sure where she stood with him, but she knew her own mind. For the first time since Charlie Gledhill, she was in love.

The next time she had a moment alone with Wal they were walking along the water's edge at Bondi, a sky full of pink clouds making everything look soft. Up ahead the rocks at the end of the beach invited two people who had an understanding to take a few moments for themselves. He moved to take her hand. Look, Wal, she said, I'm not sure about this.

You've met someone, haven't you, he said. He could see the answer in her face. Has he asked you to marry him?

No, she said. Taking a bit of a chance, aren't I? But I thought I'd better tell you, because if he asks I'm going to say yes.

Wal stopped walking. All right, Nance, he said. He turned away, left her there at the edge of the foam.

The next Sunday when she came as usual for lunch at the Glendons' he was there, because he had nowhere else to be. But he wouldn't look at her or speak to her. Maggie and Mrs Glendon were cool. Nance was stiff with the misery of having let down people who'd been good to her. She knew, though, that marrying Wal would be a mistake. Whatever happened with Ken, she knew now that she was looking for something Wal would never be able to give her.

Ken asked her home for Sunday lunch. She knew he was anxious when he went into some detail about what to expect. He had two brothers and two sisters. The family lived in the best part of Strathfield, in Sydney's inner west, in what Ken called *Anglophile bourgeois splendour*. Dad's never been to England, he said. But when he talks about going Home, he means England. Ours is a home of the Yorkshire pudding and the stiff upper lip.

Prosperous though they were, they'd fallen from an even higher level. Ken said they'd owned the main street of Auburn until the Depression had wiped out everything except the Strathfield house and his father's modest legal practice.

His mother was from Braidwood, he said, a country girl. Nance soon realised she wasn't a country girl in the same way Dolly was a country girl. Ken said that his mother claimed to be descended from Sir Richard Grenville. Nance had never heard of him, but apparently he'd fought against the Spanish Armada. Tennyson had written a poem about him. I'm afraid they're all terrible snobs, Ken said. In fact, the original Grenville was a convict, but Mum won't believe it.

They'll think I'm a gold digger, Nance thought.

At least I can say Dad's a farmer. Sounds better than a publican. Then she was ashamed of the thought.

As Mrs Gee was saying the words of welcome she was glancing at Nance's shoes and the gloves she was taking off. Nance knew she hadn't missed the mended finger of the glove, would know to a penny what the shoes cost. She'd pictured Mr Gee as a dominating sort but he turned out to be a kindly shy man rumbling away into his chin. He was the one who made sure she had a cushion at her back. Guessed she wasn't used to grace and gave her warning while she was unfolding her napkin, ironed on one side, she noticed. Now, if everyone's ready, I'll say grace. Ken's silver napkin ring was engraved with his initials in a forest of curlicues. Hers was blank, but it was solid silver.

At the start she got Ken's brothers mixed up, which was Peter and which was Dick? They were in their flannels, on their way to a match at King's, where they'd gone to school. So was Ken the only one clever enough for Fort Street, she wondered, or was there some other reason why they'd economised with him? Peter and Dick were big fair handsome men, as different from dark narrow Ken as possible. It was easy to imagine the tennis parties in Strathfield and those cheerful brothers always getting the girls.

The sisters had been debutantes. There were silver-framed photos of them in white, curtseying. The older one, Babs, admired Nance's earrings but they both knew they were only paste. Bud was full of having been to dinner with some people called Menzies the night before. Nance thought, Could she possibly mean the prime minister? Like the brothers, the sisters were beautiful, confident, with that private-school poise, and a future in front of them of prosperous husbands and well-brought-up children.

After lunch Ken and Nance escaped to a park down the road. Sorry, Ken said. Bit of an ordeal, isn't it. He touched her arm for a moment. Nance, you're an unusual woman, he said. Having a profession and so on. They admire you for that.

He hesitated.

As I do, Nance, he said. You know that, don't you. Admire...esteem... He was turned away so she only caught the words sideways. She wanted him to say it plainly: I admire you! I esteem you! That could even be Strathfield-speak for *I love you!* But the moment passed and he took his hand away.

Having seen Ken at home she felt she could make some sense of his contradictions. He was from that King-and-Empire world, but he didn't want to be. He had a family, but he wasn't part of it. The comedown of the Depression had made his family cling to a world that was disappearing, but it had made him rethink the failed old truths. He knew how to be witty but not how to be warm and spontaneous: no wonder, being the odd man out in the family.

And Nance could see why he liked her. He talked about working people, the ones born without privilege:

well, she was one of them. She was a modern professional woman, independent in every way. She couldn't be more different from his sisters. She was part of the world of the future, not the faded past, but at the same time she was presentable enough to meet his family.

She'd said no to Charlie Gledhill for what had seemed good reasons. Ken was another chance to spend her life with a man who could offer her ideas and action. She knew he liked her. She was willing to take on trust that *admire* and *esteem* were code for something more heartfelt. She'd have to make the running but she wasn't too proud for that. She had enough warmth and spontaneity for both of them, until he got the hang of it. We've both been compressed, she thought. Together we can expand into our proper shapes.

The families met for the first time at the wedding. It was the eighth of May 1940. Dolly was wearing a nice dress from Cohen's in Tamworth but next to Mrs Gee's it looked gaudy. Her voice was a bit too high, her comments on the loveliness of the day and the splendour of the flower arrangements too forceful. Bert wore the suit he'd bought in the glory days of the Cally. That time was ten years gone and the suit hung loose on him, shiny around the knees.

Dick and Peter were handsome in their officer's uniforms, although to Nance's eye Frank was more handsome than either of Ken's brothers, and she was proud to introduce him. She watched them shaking hands outside the church, Frank's rough hand and Ken's soft one. She loved bringing them together, these two men who were the most important people in her life, but with the helpless knowledge that they had so little in common. There was a pause before they both started talking about how lucky they'd been with the weather.

NANCE, 1929. 'I was seventeen when I was sent away to Sydney. Mum was anxious to be rid of me and I thought going to Sydney would be an adventure.'

CHARLIE Gledhill with his mother-in-law, early 1930s.

NANCE at the Enmore Pharmacy, 1930. 'Pharmacy was seven days a week and a fortnight's holiday a year. It was absolute slavery. I can't tell you how much I hated it. But when I dared to voice a very mild and nervous complaint I was quickly reminded how lucky I was—after all, I had a job.'

Materia Medica, 1931

MATERIA Medica, 1931:
students and instructors.

*Reproduced courtesy of the
University of Sydney Archives
(G3/224/1854).*

NANCE in clothes swapped with Rete and Molly, 1932. 'It was the very depths of the Depression, and getting dressed up probably meant putting another pair of shoes on. Clothes were something you couldn't think about. If you started to feel you wanted clothes you got a bit downhearted.'

ON the Hawkesbury, 1931: Nance on right, Meg Naughton centre. 'Some of us from the hostel would go out together on a Sunday—it didn't cost you anything, only your fare. But I had to watch the time because I'd have to be back in the shop at six o'clock.'

AT Bondi Beach, about 1938. 'I could have married Wal, or Jake. I was considering both but without really loving them.'

NANCE at Manly with her apprentice, 1936.

LEAVING Certificate class, Fort Street Boys' High 1932. Kenneth Grenville Gee at far left of front row.

WITH a friend in the city, 1939. 'I thought I liked Wal enough. I agreed to marry him one New Year's Eve after we'd had a few drinks. It wasn't a proper engagement. But a definite understanding.'

SERGEANT Walter Maxwell Russell, 1940. 'When the war started, Max joined the Army and went to the Middle East. There was all that business with Crete and he was wounded there. Then he got typhoid. We thought he was going to die.'

BOMBARDIER Frank Alexander Russell, 1940. 'Mum made Frank feel terrible about not being at the war. He was still here and Max was going to die. So he joined up. If it hadn't been for her, he wouldn't have gone to the war.

CAPTAIN Charles Gledhill, 1941. 'As usual, telling someone what to do.'

KEN, Nance and Christopher, 1941.

NANCE and
Christopher, 1942.

STEPHEN and
Christopher at Mona
Vale Beach, about 1946.

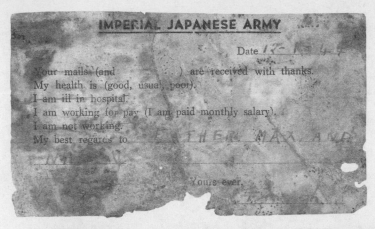

IMPERIAL JAPANESE ARMY

Date 1? - ? 4 ?

Your mails (and   ) are received with thanks.
My health is (good, usual, poor).
I am ill in hospital.
I am working for pay (I am paid monthly salary).
I am not working.
My best regards to   FATHER MAX AND

Yours ever,

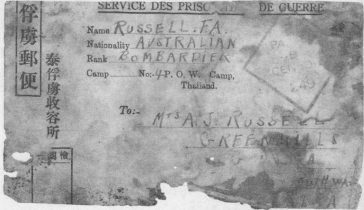

SERVICE DES PRISON   DE GUERRE

俘虜郵便

泰俘虜收容所

調檢

Name   RUSSELL.F.A.
Nationality   AUSTRALIAN
Rank   BOMBARDIER
Camp   No:- 4 P. O. W. Camp,
                     Thailand.

To:-   Mrs A. J. RUSSELL
           GREENHILLS

                     SOTH WA

FRANK'S last message, 1944.

'IN his will—clever
man—Frank left the
farm to Dad. He was
clever enough to realise
that Mum would go
and sell it. Dad worked
hard and put all he
could into it. If Frank
had come back it
would have been to
a good property.'

NINE

THEY WERE married in the morning and by evening they were in Forster, a few hours north on the train. Scanning the ads in the paper for seaside boarding houses, she'd been drawn to a French name. *L'Hirondelle*. She could try her old Tamworth High French. *Bonjour, Madame, comment allez-vous?* When she showed the ad to Ken he said, *L'Hirondelle*, that's swallow, isn't it? Sounds better in French, not so much an alcoholic's paradise. Sometimes, she thought, I could wish him less witty.

The landlady—not French—showed them to the Honeymoon Suite. The double bed looked enormous after the single beds Nance was used to. She was ready to give Ken a wink, but the landlady was showing him the washbasin in the corner behind the curtain. At dinner the other guests twinkled and smiled. As soon as the jam roll and custard was finished it was clear that they expected the newlyweds to say goodnight.

When Ken had proposed, Nance's only worry was about her hymen. Could a man tell if you weren't a virgin? She didn't think Ken had any experience with women, but there might be some way he'd know. As far as she was concerned, she and Charlie had just done the natural thing. How Ken would feel, she didn't know. Some people thought it was terribly important for a bride to be a virgin. Once or twice she'd tried to steer the conversation around, but he was uncomfortable talking about anything personal.

To her surprise, as they were planning the wedding Ken said, We don't want children straight away, do we, Nance? What about you get one of those cap things? Someone had told him about the hymen breaking, the mess and the pain and so on. Getting fitted for the cap meant the doctor broke the hymen, so that solved his problem. It solved hers too. She felt bad not confessing. But it had only been a little while with Charlie, and it was all finished now.

It was unusual for a woman to get herself fitted for a cap. There was still a feeling that it wasn't quite nice, even for a married woman. One of the doctors at the hospital knew someone but she wondered what she'd have done if she hadn't known the right sort of doctor. And what had her mother done in the years before the cap? A respectable married woman wouldn't have gone into the pharmacy in Gunnedah and asked for the Housewife's Friend, and french letters weren't for decent married men. But having only three children, Dolly must have used something. Perhaps the sponge-on-a-string worked better than you'd think. Or she might have said no. In that case, no wonder Bert started to look somewhere else.

Leaving the doctor's with the little beige box in her handbag, Nance thought, Mine is the first generation of women, in the history of the world, to have any choice about children. All those millions of women who were nothing but baby-machines. So many of them must have been like me, wanting it both ways. Children, of course, but a life of their own too.

One thing was starting to lead to another when Nance stopped and said she'd go behind the curtain for a minute. Don't go away, she said. He didn't laugh. There wasn't much room behind the curtain and it didn't quite reach down to the floor. She kept jogging it with her elbow as she got into the new nightdress with the shoestring straps and squatted on the lino to put the cap in. It must have looked as if she was wrestling in there, and in a way she was. You had to smear special cream all over the rubber dome and then fold it in half to get it in. The cream made it slippery. She imagined it springing like a frog over the curtain. Charlie had always made a joke about getting the french letter on. But beyond the curtain the room was deadly silent.

When she came out Ken was under the bedclothes, turned away so all she could see was a striped flannelette shoulder. She switched off the light, padded over to the bed and got in. The mattress sagged as he turned to her and they rolled together into the dip. She'd never done it in a bed before, only ever on the ground with the trees overhead and the small night noises all around. Never in pitch dark before, either. There'd always been light from the stars or the moon, enough to make out the smile on a face that was close to your own.

Next morning she slipped out of bed before Ken was awake. You were supposed to douche before you took the thing out. She tried to be quiet but the room filled with little splashing noises. Then it was breakfast with everyone smiling too much and the landlady giving Ken extra bacon because he needed to keep up his strength. It was a relief to get outside.

She'd have liked them to hire a boat on the lagoon and sit beside each other, the two of them jostled together on the rocking water. But Ken wanted to fish from the beach. That meant standing in the foamy wash with her brand-new husband a little figure in the distance.

They were at Forster for a week. Every night it was the same silent business of wrestling with the cap. Every day was fishing. By the end of the week she couldn't wait to be at home. They'd rented a flat in Maroubra, not far from the hospital, upstairs on a quiet road with the hopeful name of Melody Street, where the sea breeze streamed in the windows. In their own place things would go better.

One of the things Nance had looked forward to about being married was sharing the stories of the day's events, a cheerful exchange over dinner and a few laughs to ease the way into bed. On the way home from the hospital every afternoon she'd think of something that might amuse Ken. There was always a little drama of one kind or another. The nurses were forever falling in love with the doctors and getting their hearts broken. The head wardsman was having an affair with the manager's wife and thought no one knew. A patient in the lock hospital tried to kill himself by jumping off the rocks but all he did was break his leg, so now he had a broken leg as well as syphilis!

Ken listened and smiled, but he wasn't really interested and he didn't have any stories of his own to offer in return. Oh, the usual, he'd say. Conveyancing. Probate for Miss Butler. Pretty dull stuff. She felt she was coming up against a bland blank place in him like the high unseeing side of a ship.

It was a bad time to be a solicitor. With the war on, no one was buying or selling houses, no businesses were starting up and no one was suing anyone. It was lucky that people kept dying, otherwise Ken would be making even less than he did. They'd worked out that Ken paid the rent and Nance paid for everything else. She wondered how they'd be managing if she wasn't working.

After tea Ken would get out a brief and read, the pink tape draped over his knee for tying it up again. She felt she shouldn't disturb him, so she read too, or did some sewing or knitting. Then they went to bed and read some more. She'd have a novel and Ken would have one of the dense orange-covered books that came in the mail from the Left Book Club.

Once or twice a week he'd go out after dinner. Another party meeting, he'd say, and she'd remember the men rising to their feet with the sheaf of pages and couldn't face going with him. In any case, Ken didn't seem to want her company. No, Nance, he'd say. No need for you to come. Listening to the wireless on her own she told herself that politics was his passion. It was how she'd met him. It was what she admired in him, that knowledge about the big meaning of things. She couldn't ask him to stop just because she wanted his company in the evenings.

Living together, they found their differences were more noticeable. She smoked, and he liked to boast that a cigarette had never soiled his lips. She'd grown up playing cards, but he didn't approve. She got the feeling he thought it was vulgar. She'd get out her Keats and Shakespeare and re-read those words that never lost their power but, despite his first-class honours in English, Ken wasn't interested in poetry. If he read anything that wasn't from the Left Book Club it would be what he called a *rattling good yarn* by Edgar Wallace. She came to see that, for Ken, poetry was a code you cracked to get honours in an exam, not a blazing discovery.

Everyone said that a marriage required compromise. She wasn't going to stop quoting poetry, but she didn't look to Ken to share the pleasure. She sat out on the back steps to smoke and she gave up cards.

After a time, Ken left his father's practice and set up his brass plate on a room in Maroubra. A man shouldn't play second fiddle to his father forever. All the same, Nance had seen the look on Mr Gee's face when Ken told him: too abruptly, too thanklessly. Ken could have pretended it was something they'd come to together. Could have saved the old man's pride. It was the first time she saw the steel in him.

On Friday nights a group from the Coast Hospital went out together: the other pharmacists, some of the nurses, the ward orderlies. A cheap meal, a few beers, a few laughs. Ken came once or twice, but he didn't enjoy it. No one around the table knew what a Christian Socialist was or was interested in the threat to democracy. She'd see him forcing a smile while he listened to Stan tell the one about the spider and the nun, and pushing back his cuff to glance at the time. Soon it turned out that he had to stay in the office on a Friday night, in case someone came. Stay till eight o'clock, she said. Then come along and have sweets with us. *Sweets.* In the Gee household you didn't have *sweets*, you had *dessert.* Oh, good idea, he said, but he never came.

There was no point begging or scolding. That had been her mother's way. That was no good. If a man didn't want to be with you, no amount of begging or scolding would make him. Dolly hadn't had any choice. Making life miserable for other people was the only power she had.

It was different for Nance. She wasn't dependent on a man. In fact, she thought that might be part of the problem. She'd been running her own life for so long, she was used to shaping things as she wanted. She knew that other women adapted their lives around their husbands, but she knew she couldn't. She was like those girls who learned to dance with other girls, taking turns to be the man. They never got the hang of following, once they knew what it was like to lead.

At the end of a few months she could see she wasn't going to like life with Ken. She didn't want to be on her own every night while her husband was out. Didn't want to sit stiff and uncomfortable watching him with her friends. She was happy to put away her cards and her cigarettes but Ken's indifference to poetry betrayed the depth of the gulf between them. The failure wasn't his fault and it wasn't her fault. It was that the two of them were too different. She wasn't happy and she didn't think he was either, and it was hard to imagine how things could ever get better.

It was a decision she had to make alone. There was no one to talk it over with. Her mother, with her own miserable marriage, would have nothing useful to say. Besides, she'd never warmed to Ken. *I could have told you* would hang in the air. Joan was blissfully content to be Mrs Harry Mulhall. She'd be shocked and uncomprehending. Frank would understand, she thought, but how could you talk about things like this in a letter?

She was in love with Ken, but there was steel in her

too. When you make a mistake you have to face up to it, she thought. Admit you've failed and cut your losses. I'll leave, she decided. Next weekend. Go back to the boarding house. She could imagine the fuss. Everyone would be agog. People loved a scandal. She'd have to face up to that too. It didn't work out, she'd say. No harm done and no bad feeling. She'd be so matter-of-fact, they'd soon lose interest. Two years of separation and she and Ken could get a quiet divorce. Then they could both start again.

But at work next day Joan said, Harry and I are going to Bobbin Head on Saturday, Nance, why don't you and Ken come with us?

Nance thought, I can hardly say: Well, actually, I'm going to leave my husband on Saturday. She told Joan she couldn't come because she had something to do. Joan wanted to know what, and Nance said the first thing she thought of. I've got to stay home and wash the windows.

Wash the windows! Joan laughed, but in a puzzled way.

The silliness of the excuse made Nance realise she only half meant to leave. This is a big decision, she thought. I'd better not do it unless I'm sure. Why wasn't she sure? Was this what love was, the kind of love the great writers talked about, that made you do one thing when you wanted to do another? She did love Ken, but she was strong enough to know when you should resist love. She'd resisted with Charlie Gledhill, and could do the same with Ken. No, it was something else that was keeping her in this marriage.

There was something at work in her that was stronger than all her reasons for leaving. She could feel it moving in her as it did in every kind of animal. It was the urge to have children. It wasn't about seeing babies in the street and wanting your own sweet little bundle. It wasn't about wanting someone to love you. Somehow it was less personal than any of that. It was more fundamental, like hunger or thirst. It was the primitive drive of the species.

And a child could be a new start. It might even bring them together. Without the passion-killer of ducking out to put the cap in, she and Ken might learn to relax with each other. Perhaps she could make him love her. And if none of those hopeful things happened, at least she'd have a child.

When she told Ken she wanted to start a family, he said he'd have to think about it. She'd learned that was his cautious lawyer's way. Never commit yourself. But that night in bed he made up to her and, when she went to put the cap in, he said, No, Nance, leave it.

It did seem as if things went better after that. Ken was still out two or three nights a week at meetings, but at the weekends he'd find the time for the two of them to go out together: to the Domain to listen to the speakers, or a ferry ride to Manly.

After three months she was sure. The weight of doubt and decision lifted. From now on her role was simple. All she had to do for the next six months was to be a container.

Ken hugged her when she told him, held her close the way she'd always hoped he would. After tea he put the wireless on and they foxtrotted around the kitchen, and when a slow tune came on they danced cheek to cheek. It will be all right, she thought. He'll be different now. Being a loving father will make him a loving husband.

Bert and Dolly offered their congratulations. *You'll have your dear little baby*, Dolly wrote, and didn't need to say, Even if your husband is a disappointment.

TEN

A WEEK after Ken and Nance had got back from Forster, Germany invaded France. Then it was the Dunkirk business. It looked as though Britain would fall within a month.

Frank wrote to say he'd joined up. He didn't want to, but Dolly had nagged and it was true, he said, it was a matter of all hands to the pump. There was the disaster in Europe, and then there was Japan as well, heading south through one country after another. Everyone was very sure that Australia was in no danger. The Japanese would never get past Singapore. In the cartoons they were pathetic creatures, buck-toothed and shortsighted, straining away on bicycles. The Whitehall bigwigs called them *yellow dwarf slaves*. Still, the war was too close for comfort.

Frank was made a bombardier on an anti-tank gun. There was a picture in the paper of a man sitting behind one, swivelling the barrel like a movie cameraman, with two little wheels. *There's a hole the size of a sixpence to look through,* Frank wrote. *The trick is not to do the natural, stand up to have a proper look. You only get to do that once.*

He said that his commanding officer, a good bloke by the name of Carrick, wanted him to go to NCO school and move up the ranks, but Frank wasn't interested. Plenty of chiefs already, he said. I'll stay an Indian.

After North Africa, Max had fought in Greece but the Germans had beaten them there. They'd retreated to Crete until the Germans got there too. Now they were in Egypt, and Max had got typhoid. He was going to be invalided home but they thought he'd die.

Even Charlie Gledhill joined up, over in England. He sent Nance a snap of himself in uniform, some kind of naval doctor. *Dear Nance,* he wrote, *I was glad to hear you were married. Your husband is a lucky man. I think of you often and always with the warmest feelings.* In the photo he was caught pointing out of frame in the middle of saying something. On the back he'd written, *As usual, telling someone what to do.* Yes, she thought. He knows himself and knows me too. Two bossy people in the one marriage: that would never have worked.

No one handed out white feathers these days, but as the war news got worse Nance wondered how Ken felt, an able-bodied young man not in uniform. People glanced at them when they were out together. He didn't seem to notice, but what was he thinking? He never talked about joining up. It was as if somehow it didn't apply to him.

Nance didn't feel she could talk to him about it. Imagine if she did, and he felt pressured to join up, and got killed!

In her letters Dolly never missed a chance to say how lucky Nance was not to have a husband away fighting, the way most women did. All Nance could do was put on a brave face and ignore the hints.

When Frank enlisted, Dolly left the farm at Guyra. There was work for everyone now, even a half-educated woman of sixty. She had a string of casual jobs in Sydney: cook in a hospital, housemaid in a hotel. Easy work, good money, room and board thrown in. For the first time in her life she could do as she pleased, beholden to no man.

Bert left Mittagong and came up to look after Green Hills while Frank was away. After so many pubs leased and sold, after a fortune made and lost, it was back to ploughing and shearing. His letters to Nance were full of his plans. He was going to improve the pasture and buy a good ram. *Do my very best for Frank*, he said. *Make it a showplace by the time he gets back.*

She wasn't going to say anything at the hospital about the baby until she had to. War or no war, a woman with a job was already bad in the eyes of a lot of people. A married woman working was worse. A pregnant woman working was unheard of. She'd work until she couldn't hide it any more, and build up a bit in the bank.

It was humbling, being pregnant. Things were happening in her body that were nothing to do with any decision she made. There was a surrender to the process, a great passive peace that came from submitting to her body and all the things it knew that she didn't.

She'd always thought art was the great teacher about life. That moment with the Enmore tram had proved it for her. But none of the great writers talked about the biggest drama of all. A woman feeling a new person grow inside her had no words to understand it with. It wasn't the subject of a single sonnet or novel. You were alone with it, other than the commonplaces that other women could offer: the old woman on the bus who assured her that when she started sweeping the yard it meant her time was come, or the neighbour who felt her bump and proclaimed that the baby was a girl.

She and Ken were on the ferry one Sunday when they met two men who Ken seemed to know. There was something funny in the way the three of them greeted one another, a hesitation and then an overdone heartiness. Jack Wishart, my wife Nance, Ken said. Alan Thistlethwaite, my wife Nance. She smiled. What a peculiar name Thistlethwaite was. He must have to write small to fit it on his cheques, and did the woven-labels people charge extra for so many letters? The men did that little not-quite bow that men did to women, and to her surprise Ken put his arm around her. Nance is a pharmacist, he said. Works at the Coast Hospital.

Oh, the Coast, the one called Thistlethwaite said. You'd know Miss Young, she's the librarian out there. We're friends of hers, aren't we, Jack?

She knew Miss Young, a quiet watchful woman too old and spinsterish for there to be any hanky-panky with either of these men. There was something going on, though. How men loved their little secret games!

She and Ken strolled like a courting couple along the Corso.

Those fellers, they're in with the Trotskyites, Ken said. But keep it under your hat, Nance. It's an illegal organisation.

Funny, Nance thought, you'd never pick either of those men for a red.

Matter of fact, they run it, Ken said. They've invited me in, Nance, and I said yes. Joined up last week.

How do you mean, Ken, joined, she said, thinking for a confused moment he'd enlisted.

I've been considering it for quite a time, Ken said. The Labor Party's moribund and the Trotskyites have got it right. I applied and I was accepted. They've given me a party name for security. Comrade Roberts.

Comrade Roberts! What, a made-up name? She started to laugh but stopped.

Nance, this is a dangerous game, he said. He was talking low and glancing around, though no one was watching. They call us subversives. He put an ironic spin on the word. And they're right, Nance. In fact we're more than that. We're revolutionaries.

She didn't know whether to laugh or be appalled. Comrade Roberts! Revolution! She still only half understood.

So you're a communist, she said, but he made a derisive noise.

Not communist! Not those Stalinist boobies. We Trotskyites follow a different kind of socialism, Nance. We're the true socialists. I'll explain it all later.

So that was what all those meetings were, she said. Not Labor Party.

Oh, the Labor Party expelled me, he said, and she heard the pride. Lang expelled me for moving too far to the Left.

Not the Labor Party! All this time—how long had it been?—he'd let her think the endless meetings were more of Lang and the point-of-order types, when he'd been travelling on a secret inner journey. No wonder her little stories about the broken hearts at the Coast had never interested him. Was it better to have a husband who was never home because he didn't love you, or because he was a revolutionary?

And who am I to doubt, she thought. I don't know anything about this Trotsky thing. She'd picked Ken and not Wal Glendon because Ken was interested in ideas. Now he was acting because of an idea. He had the brains and the passion to be a leader of men.

I'm proud of you, darling, she said, and kissed him. He didn't like that, kissing in public. But when she took his hand he didn't take it away.

Later she asked him what it was all about. Why Trotsky? Ken went all the way back to the tsars to make sure she got the full picture. He relished rolling out Trotsky's real name: Lev Davidovich Bronstein. He explained that he'd taken the name Leon Trotsky when he became a revolutionary. She started to understand that the Trotskyites were a special sort of communist. In fact they seemed to hate the other communists even more than they hated the capitalists.

Ken was eager, explaining it all to her. She thought she might be getting the hang of making marriage work. You had to be interested and you had to not know too much.

He gave her what he called his bible to read: *The Permanent Revolution* by Leon Trotsky. It wasn't as hard to read as she'd feared. Everything she'd learned from those miserable years of the Depression—all the unfairness, loss and tragedy—had nothing to do with bad luck or even bad management. According to Trotsky, the machine of capitalism was to blame. It was a machine designed to keep working people on the bottom and the bosses on top. She'd seen it in her own life: no one got ahead working for someone else. The people who owned the business would always be the winners. Her parents had thought they could borrow their way into joining those winners, but in the end the bank had won. Trotsky was saying that there was no use tinkering with the system. You had to undo it all and start again.

She thought on the whole Trotsky's ideas were sensible, but now and then he'd come out with something shocking. *We were never concerned with the Kantian-priestly and vegetarian-Quaker prattle about the 'sacredness of human life'*, she read, and recoiled. That's where I part company from Trotsky, she thought. I don't have all the words, but I know I'm right about that. Human life *is* sacred.

Next time Nance passed Miss Young in the hallway at the hospital she said, Oh, Miss Young, I met a friend of yours recently, a Mr Thistlethwaite. A friend of my husband. I believe they have an associate in common, name of Leon.

Miss Young smiled and gave her the shadow of a wink. Oh yes, she said, I've heard that Mr Gee knows Leon. Again the smile, and Nance went on her way understanding the thrill of talking in code. It was as if you were two people at once, twice as alive.

She saw that Ken had always been the outsider: out of place in his family, out of place in a profession that didn't interest him, out of place even in their marriage. Being part of this secret elite was the outsider's way of joining. He was a man newly energised, brought to life by that inner coiled spring of passion.

He explained why he hadn't enlisted: this was the bosses' war, over national boundaries that were part of the machinery of capitalism. The international proletariat had no borders. If all the world's workers rose up in what Trotsky called the Terminal Crisis, there'd be no more war. The Dictatorship of the Proletariat would forge a better world and the future would be glorious.

Nance said yes, but in the meantime Germany and Japan were knocking over country after country, and looked like taking the whole world before the Terminal Crisis. All the more reason to be vigorous in spreading the word, was Ken's answer, and be disciplined in resisting the call to arms. *Not a Man, Not a Ship, Not a Gun for the Bosses' War.*

He had an answer for every argument. She wasn't convinced, but she was silenced. It was his profession, after all, she thought: finding reasons to support whatever case he was making. And there was always the chance that he was right. Revolution had happened in Russia, when it must have looked impossible there. The incredible thought was that it could happen in Australia too.

At the Domain he introduced her to some of the other comrades gathered under the Communist League banner. Jim McClelland looked dapper even in a worker's cap and John Kerr, one of Ken's classmates from Fort Street, was an imposing figure with a great shock of thick hair. Ken called him an *intellectual titan*. Like Ken, they were both lawyers. Guido Baracchi kissed her hand in an elaborate way. She noticed his beautiful Italian shoes. Not the shoes of a working man! Laurie Short, a nuggetty energetic union organiser, was the only genuine proletarian.

There was a back-to-front aristocracy among the revolutionaries. At the top were the proletarians like Laurie. At the bottom were the recruits from nice middle-class homes. As a pharmacist, on her feet all day, she was certainly a worker. But a pharmacist was usually a business person too. The comrades were polite to her, but she wasn't one of them.

In any case, women didn't count among the Fourth International, Sydney Branch. Ken told her—several times—what Trotsky had said when asked about the role of women in the revolution. Ken quoted him as saying, *They should be rooted on the workshop floor.*

Ken took his turn up on the stepladder in the Domain. When someone heckled him, she'd see the light in his eye as he thought of a clever put-down. The crowd would laugh and the heckler would turn sullen. Well done, comrade, McClelland or Short would say, clapping Ken on the back.

There was something about the business that didn't convince her. She didn't believe Ken really cared about the workers. After all, real workers were those people he didn't want to go to dinner with. He'd never worked seven days a week at a job he hated but couldn't afford to leave. She had the private disloyal thought that, for Ken, revolution was a complicated game he was good at, a secret and dangerous game that got the blood racing.

By the time Nance was too pregnant to hide the fact, she was happy to leave the Coast Hospital. They did a whip-round and got her a second-hand Singer, such a generous gift she was in tears. The tears were also for saying goodbye to her old life. Once the baby was born she'd be bound to this new human being in a way she'd never been bound to anyone before. The tears were for the end of a certain kind of selfishness.

And for her independence. She'd always had her own money and had taken her independence for granted. When she first left work she kept that independence by dipping into her savings to buy the food and pay the bills, but soon realised she couldn't keep it up. She had to accept that from now on all her money came from Ken. He was generous with the housekeeping money and never queried when she came to him for extra. But she was conscious of the way money could change the shape of a relationship. If Ken wanted to stay at home on a Saturday afternoon rather than take her to the pictures, behind their disagreement was the shadow of an unspoken contract: It's my money you're living off, so we'll do what I want. When he made up to her in bed and she wasn't in the mood, there it was again: My money, my right.

The baby was jumping around now, keeping her awake at night. How strange it was to feel a little foot-shaped bulge under the covering of her own flesh. It was a cliché to call it a miracle, but that's what it was. Ken talked about the proletariat being the midwives of history. This was no metaphor. It was the thing itself.

She'd wondered how she'd know when the moment came, but at the first pain there was no doubt. Vast stretches of time spoke to her through her body. She was every mother since Eve. Every one of those bodies had begun the long business of expelling the new being that had grown inside the old one. She had a long but uncomplicated labour and at the end of it there he was, the person she'd been waiting to meet. It was the day after her twenty-ninth birthday, the twenty-sixth of August 1941. He was a solid bundle, not fragile as she'd feared. Her arms knew exactly what to do.

Once mother and baby were nicely arranged, the nurse let Ken come in. He smiled and touched her shoulder, and held the baby for a few minutes. She was glad he was there. Still, something in her had shifted. Ken might never be the husband she'd hoped for. But it wasn't the two of them any more, a husband and wife going along in a lopsided way. There was someone else in the world who mattered more than either of them.

ELEVEN

TIME HAD a different meaning after Christopher was born. It wasn't measured by the clock, but by the baby. Time to feed him, to change his nappy, to play with him, to take him out in the pram. Nance loved to watch him sleeping, loved to feel him feeding and know that her body was all he needed. It was as if she'd gone to another country where all the big things became small things, and the small things were all that mattered.

There was a little garden at the back of the flats and she loved to put him on a rug there and laugh with him at the new wonders of his world. Fingers! Leaves! Birds! When she leaned in to kiss his fat cheek she could see herself tiny in his eyes. It was a bond more profound than anything she could have imagined, frightening in its power.

Ken loved the baby too, made a popping noise with a finger in his cheek that made Christopher laugh.

Carried him around the room, jiggling him and singing, *This is the way the ladies ride, ladies ride, ladies ride.* She'd think, He's changed, it's going to be different. But soon he'd hand Christopher back and it would be as it always was. He had papers to go through, or a meeting to go to.

At work every day, Ken didn't have the timeless moments with Christopher that she loved so much. Nance would have felt sorry for him if she thought he missed them. He loved his son, she knew. But she'd come to see that something in her husband was stunted. Grand, overwhelming feelings frightened him. He was content with something smaller. Perhaps I can't blame him, she thought. It's that cold upbringing he had. It's left him embarrassed by emotions. Having feelings meant going into some part of himself he wanted to keep hidden.

He was out more and more with the comrades. Took elaborate precautions, setting off briskly from the front gate towards La Perouse when she knew he was really going to Paddington, his Trotsky papers rolled up in a newspaper so he could get rid of them quickly. She thought all the cloak-and-dagger stuff was ridiculous until one night he came home shaking. He and another man had been putting pamphlets in people's letterboxes along Selwyn Street in Paddington when the coppers were suddenly there. Tipped off, Ken said. He legged it, got away down a dunny lane, strolled out to Oxford Street and jumped on the first bus. They got the other man, put the cuffs on him. He'd do time. Distributing subversive literature. Six months and a five-hundred-pound fine.

She knew Ken wouldn't have wanted to be caught. Imagine him in a cell with some burglar, and a bucket in the corner! At the same time, she thought there was a flicker of him wishing that he hadn't been so smart in getting away.

Christopher was two months old when his uncle Frank's unit was sent to Timor. Three months later, the impossible happened: Singapore fell to the Japanese. It was gone, and with it more than a hundred thousand captured soldiers.

Then the news came that the Japanese had taken Timor. That was all the paper said: *Japanese forces landed on Timor Island yesterday, according to reports from Tokio. Australian troops there would be expelled.* Then there was no more mention of Timor. Frank and all the men with him had vanished into a great silence.

Now the Japanese were bombing Darwin. The *Sydney Morning Herald* issued a special call for *unity, self-sacrifice and confidence in facing the enemy* and printed a booklet, *What to Do in the Case of an Invasion.*

Nance woke up every morning with the thought, Is he still alive? The war became personal, every action a bargain with fate.

One Saturday afternoon, out walking with Christopher, she passed a Catholic church and glanced in through its wide-open doors. It was full of people waiting to go into confession. There was a sense of light and warmth and a cheerful family mood. Her feet took her in.

She joined people at one of the side altars, thinking from the crowd that this must be the saint who looked after soldiers. The statue above the altar was like the ones she'd scoffed at years ago, that sure-of-herself schoolgirl. She didn't know whether she believed or what she believed, but she needed to be here, with all these other people looking for comfort.

An older woman turned away from the altar and made a place for her. Nance saw her tears, put out a hand and touched her arm. Took a candle and lit it from one that was already burning. Christopher twisted in her arms towards the lights, the dozens of frail bending flames, bearing all those prayers upwards.

Coming out she felt less alone. Others, longing for their own soldiers to be safe, would light their candle from hers, and the murmuring mass of longings would become one river of entreaty. *Keep him safe*.

When she got home Ken was at the kitchen table reading a newspaper. She knew it must be the *Socialist Worker* because that was the only paper he bothered with now. He called the others *pabulum*. She'd had to ask him what it meant. It was part of the Trotsky language, like *Fourth International* and *Dictatorship of the Proletariat*. She thought he was probably right about the newspapers, they put the best face on things, but they had to because otherwise everyone would give up, and God knows what would happen then, to Frank and to all of them.

She saw the headline where Ken was reading— 'Don't Fight the Capitalists' War!'—and felt a spurt of rage.

Ken, she said, Max and Frank are over there. You know that. My brothers. They need more men to go and help them.

Your brothers are brave men, he said. Honourable men.

You think they're fools, don't you, she said. Fighting the bosses' war.

Oh, not fools, Nance, he said. Only, well, naïve. I'm sorry about Frank, but the sooner one side or the other wins this war, the better. The worse things are, the sooner they'll be better.

She was so angry she couldn't speak. She went into the bedroom and stood at the open window, trying to breathe. The Trotsky idea might be right in some ways. She knew all the arguments about the bosses' war. But what Ken said about her brothers was like the *vegetarian-Quaker prattle* thing. How could he be so calm about it, so smug? She was ashamed for him, and for herself too. This was the man she'd married, a man lacking in proper feelings. She didn't want to spend her life with a man like that.

As she jiggled Christopher and shushed into his ear she realised how narrow her choices were. She might have left, that day she'd said she had to wash the windows, but having a child changed everything. At a pinch you could live in a boarding house with a baby, but how would you pay the rent? If you went back to work to pay the rent, who would look after the baby?

Meg had called marriage legalised prostitution and

she was nearly right, except it wasn't marriage that made it so, it was having a child. How ruthless nature is, she thought, that the joy of having a child makes you willing to walk into that trap.

On impulse she decided to visit Bert at the farm in Guyra. She didn't know if she was ready to leave Ken for good, only that she couldn't go on sitting in that flat with him reading about the capitalists' war. She might stay for a week, or she could keep extending the visit until it was a new life. There was nowhere else she could go.

Bert was pleased to see her but he wasn't going to change his routines. Every morning he harnessed up the Clydesdales and went out ploughing. He didn't believe in tractors, thought they compressed the soil. He'd come back from the paddocks when it got too dark to see, eat his chops and potatoes, have a few glasses of whisky and go to bed. He and Nance didn't talk much. They were both thinking about Frank but there was no point in talking about him, because they didn't know if he was dead or alive. Nothing else seemed worth remarking on.

Green Hills was ten miles from town. Bert had a truck but she'd never learned to drive and he didn't have time to teach her. There were no neighbours, no shops down the road, nowhere to take the baby in the pram even if she'd had the pram with her. Once a week Bert drove to Guyra for supplies. Nance went with him, gabbled at Mrs Mackie in the grocer's for the pleasure of having another human to talk to. At least out in the paddocks Bert had the Clydesdales. They were good listeners.

When a letter came from Ken she ripped open the envelope and read it right there in the post office in front of old Mr Moorhouse. She'd left no hint that her trip to Guyra was anything more than a visit, but his letter was full of warmth and promises. He'd be different, he'd be a better husband, he'd make her happy. She thought, Never underestimate this man.

She didn't believe him, because she didn't think he could change the way he was made, any more than she could. Yes, he'd make an effort for a while, as he did if they had a row about something. He'd buy her a bunch of flowers and for a day or two he'd make a great splashing to-do of the washing-up, sit with her after tea and make her laugh. She knew now that the funny stories were carefully worked up. He'd think of the story and then lead the conversation around so he could tell it. His parents' house had never been called Banksias. Still, even after she knew his charm was a fib, she found him hard to resist when he laid himself out to please. If only he could understand that she didn't want a performance. What she wanted was for him to talk to her, ordinary conversation about real things. People, and feelings, and what it meant to be alive in the world.

It wouldn't be any different in Sydney, but she couldn't stay at Green Hills. She had to write back and say she was coming home, because what else could she do?

At last a card came from Frank.

> *I am now in a Japanese prisoner of war camp in Java.*
> *My health is excellent. The Japanese treat us well so don't*
> *worry and never feel uneasy. Hope all well. Write soon.*
> *Love, Frank.*

It was Frank's writing but the words were someone else's. *Never feel uneasy.* That was out of a phrasebook. The men must have been told what to write, she thought. Still, behind the words was the only message that mattered: when the card was written, Frank was alive.

The war was going so badly that no one made a fuss when the government started conscription, all able-bodied males between eighteen and thirty-five unless they worked in an exempt occupation. The conscripts were only supposed to fight on Australian territory, but New Guinea was Australian territory and so they were there, fighting the Japanese. Men who weren't fighting had to register with Manpower. Manpower could send you to work anywhere.

Ken was beside himself. *An outrageous erosion of liberty,* he called it. She took him on. She didn't care, she said. Not if it helped them win the war and get her brothers home safe. He looked at her in surprise and she realised she'd been shouting. But he wouldn't yield. Thinking like hers was what they counted on, he said.

Nance caught herself banging the saucepan down on the stove in frustration and remembered her mother at Rothsay. She began to look forward to the letter that Manpower would send Ken. No matter what he says about the running dogs of imperialism, she told herself, he won't be able to avoid the war now.

He came to her one afternoon and said, I've closed the practice, Nance. Been offered a job on the waterfront.

The waterfront, she said. Did Manpower come?

Not Manpower, he said. The comrades arranged it. I'm to be a boilermaker's labourer, Nance.

Ken, a soft-handed intellectual, being a boiler-maker's labourer! It seemed ridiculous, although it made some kind of sense when he explained. As a Trotskyite he had to throw his lot in with the workers. The proletariat. The revolution wasn't going to start in a suburban solici-tor's office, after all.

He didn't believe in the capitalists' war, so he couldn't let himself be put to work making bullets. The comrades had made sure he'd be working on merchant ships, not warships. He was as proud as if he'd been made a judge. Saw himself, she realised, as a latter-day Trotsky: an intellectual who wasn't afraid to live out the reality of his beliefs.

She was already imagining the pity she'd get from everyone. One day the wife of a solicitor, the next of an unskilled labourer. But she wasn't going to let them pity her. She'd rather be thought a fool. She came up with all sorts of ways to square it with herself. She should be proud of a husband who was willing to get his hands dirty, doing hard honest labour. And even if she didn't agree with them, she had to respect his convictions. After all, she'd come back from Guyra knowing she had to make a go of the marriage, and standing by your husband was part of that. She told herself that it was the side of Ken she liked best: not to do the ordinary, never to swim with the current.

All the same, a little voice deep inside reminded her that boilermaking was an exempt occupation. Oh, you sneak, Ken!

The comrades had organised for him to work on a French ship, the *Ville d'Amiens*. He got a boilersuit and some strong boots and the first day she made him a couple of sandwiches and a thermos of tea and tried not to think how the brand-new boilersuit gave the game away. She should have rolled it in the dirt and washed it a few times.

He came home that night full of what he'd seen. She'd never seen him so excited. His job was to grasp a red-hot rivet with tongs, slide it into the hole in the steel, and hold it up while Big Andy bashed the end flat. He showed her the red blisters on his hands. His innocent pride in being a worker made something curdle in her, thinking of all the men and women in the world for whom heavy dangerous work was all that stood between them and hunger.

As the days passed his innocence turned to a sly knowingness, an insider's world-weary cynicism about the foreign land of the proletariat. It was a terrific discovery that the workers had tricks to beat the bosses. At the start he'd worked too hard, too eagerly. Make a show, Ken, they'd told him. Just make a show. That meant you worked when the boss was about, and when he wasn't you found a corner where you could sit and yarn. One man had a second job where he worked the night shift, and spent the day asleep on a little nest of blankets on top of one of the *Ville d'Amiens*' boilers.

Ken interpreted the glee that the workers took in cheating the boss as a sign that they were ripe for revolution. She didn't argue, but she thought it was rather that Ken was seeing for the first time the world she'd come from, a world where you had to look out for yourself. No money in the bank, no grand slogans. If you could get away with cheating the boss in some small way, that was your little bit of power, the only kind you'd ever have. Whereas, in truth, Ken was playing at being a worker.

He told her that on Friday afternoons, when the foreman was sleeping off his lunch, some of the men went across the road to where the tarts advertised they were open for business by hanging a pair of long-johns out the window. The idea excited him. Not so much the sex, she thought, but the long-johns. The code. Being in the know.

She didn't ask, and he didn't say, but she doubted that they would have asked him along. He thought he was one of them but she was pretty sure he wasn't. He made her laugh with his stories of Big Andy and Little Andy and the others, but was Big Andy at that moment making his wife laugh with stories of the fellow who'd come to work in a spotless new boilersuit and didn't know which end of a spanner was up?

To be closer to Ken's work they left Maroubra and took a flat in Cremorne, where he could get the ferry straight across to the docks. One night they were woken by a great booming, heavy enough for the teacups to rattle in the cupboard. She knew straight away it was bombs. It was impossible, bombs were what happened in London, but she ran into the little room where Christopher was asleep and snatched him up. If there were bombs, even dream bombs, she was going to die with him.

Next morning it was on the radio. The Japanese had got into Sydney Harbour and torpedoed the warships at Woolloomooloo. War, unreal, in black and white on the newsreels, was suddenly among them. The harbour, shifting and sparkling, was like a wound where infection could pour in.

Mrs Gee rang up. Nance had never heard her voice unsteady with feeling before. You've got to come to us, Nance, she kept saying. You'll be safer here. Nance held Christopher in the crook of her arm, thinking, Yes, we have to go. Refugees, like those lines of people she'd seen on the newsreels labouring along with suitcases. How do you decide what to take? A warm coat and nappies for the baby, or the family photos and the watch you were given for your twenty-first?

Once they were at Strathfield she could see that

Mrs Gee was sorry she'd spoken. She wasn't a woman who liked babies, had no patience with a doting mother. Oh, let him cry! she said. You're spoiling him! It was just the four of them in the house, plus the baby, because Peter and Dick were away at the war, Babs had got married and Bud was always out, no one seemed to know quite where.

Ken's parents were bewildered by their son's Trotskyite convictions and especially by the boilermaking. His father scrupulously never reproached, but his mother wasn't shy about telling Ken he was throwing himself away on this communist nonsense. At dinner, across the expanse of mahogany, Ken turned a blank surface to what was going on around him. She had to admire his ability to withdraw. Wished she could do the same sometimes.

For her there was no escape, alone in the house with her mother-in-law. The best part of the day was after lunch, when she could put Christopher in the pram and get out into the empty streets of Strathfield. She'd walk until Christopher cried to be fed, and even then she'd find the long way back home.

They took the first flat they saw in the area, the back half of a house in nearby Ashfield, with gaunt gloomy rooms that never got warm. Ashfield was a poor man's Strathfield, the streets narrower, the houses smaller, but the same privet hedges and crazy-paving. In Ken's terms, Strathfield was bourgeois but Ashfield was the even more contemptible petty-bourgeois, an awful secretive genteel poverty that strained to pretend.

But he didn't care where they lived. The Trotsky meetings took all his time when he wasn't at work. There were three or four a week now. Sometimes the comrades met at the Ashfield flat. Only members were allowed to be at the meeting, so Nance sat in the kitchen listening to the murmur behind the closed door. She was supposed to answer the bell if anyone rang and keep them talking while the comrades got away out the back.

One night the meeting was longer than usual. When everyone had gone, Ken came out with a bundle of papers and an anxious look about his mouth. The papers would land them in jail if they were found, he said. He'd been given the job of keeping them safe.

Why does it have to be you, Ken? she said. Have they forgotten you've got a wife and child? She heard her anger and knew how thin her layer of tolerance was.

Ken was trying to pull up a corner of the lino. In one of his Edgar Wallace stories the lino would have peeled back and the boards would have been conveniently loose, but the Ashfield place was solidly built. She emptied the biscuits out of the Arnott's tin and pushed it at him. Put them in there and bury them under the house, Ken, she said. I'm not going to have those things in here!

TWELVE

DOLLY GOT a card from Frank, from Number 4 Camp, Thailand, and sent it on to Nance. It was printed, with alternatives that you could cross out. *My health is good / usual / poor. I am working for pay / I am not working.* His signature and the address on the front were the only words he was allowed to write.

Mrs A. J. Russell, Green Hills, Guyra, NSW, Australia. Nance stared at the blue ink and thought, Oh, how he must have longed to be there as he wrote each of those words. In his mind's eye he'd have seen the way the land fell away from the back of the house, the green hills making a lovely view down the valley, the pine trees he'd planted as a windbreak and the soft curve in the drive as you turned in from the road. It was all still there and, for a moment, writing the words, he would have been, too, breathing the cool air of home.

Max was back in Australia and she went to see

him in hospital. The typhoid had gone into his spine somehow and his whole body was in plaster. They thought he'd never walk properly again. He was still the cheerful warm-hearted brother he'd always been. She sat by the bed and held his hand while he dozed, remembering how she'd had a billycart at Camden and he'd always pestered her for a turn. At Temora the three of them had got on Frank's pony and gone out to the old Mother Shipton mine to look for gold. At Cronulla they'd had those pancakes in the bush.

When he was awake he told her about the fighting he'd done. Libya was all right, he said, but Greece was a debacle. It was a word he must have heard someone else say. We were tricked, Nance, he said. The Poms told us it would be all right, we went in like mugs, got cut to ribbons.

There'd been no hint of any of that in the newspapers. The news was always good and, if it couldn't be made good, then we'd *made the enemy pay a heavy price*. But Max said the Germans had rolled right over them. Then when they'd been evacuated to Crete it had been a right old mess, he said. There was nothing about that in the paper, either. What was the point of reading the news and talking about it with other people whose information was as misleading as your own? Ken was right. It was all hot air to make people go on thinking they were winning.

She'd put up with not being able to buy any prunes for Christopher, thinking dried fruit was one more small sacrifice that civilians had to make. Then on one of her visits Max told her the full story. It made her cranky enough to write a letter to the paper.

> *Dear Sir,*
> *Some time ago all the prunes and apricots in Australia were commandeered for the Army. While the attempt to improve the diet of the soldier is to be commended, surely it need not be at the expense of babies. We hear on all sides that the soldiers are heartily tired of prunes and apricots and one can readily imagine the waste that ensues. Would it not be more sensible to release enough for the babies and make up any deficiency to the soldiers with other fruits as they become plentiful, e.g. apples at present?*
>
> > *N. Gee, Ashfield*
> > *29th May 1942*

She showed it to Ken before she sent it. Very good, Nance, he said, but you know the papers aren't interested in prunes. She sent it anyway, and a week later there it was in the *Sydney Morning Herald*. Your name in print at last, Ken said. Not *at last*, she said, trying to keep the annoyance out of her voice. On the first try!

Max finally got over the typhoid apart from a stiffness in his back and they sent him to Bathurst on light duties. He wrote to Nance every month. The letters were always the same: he hoped Nance was as well as he was, the weather was fine or it looked as if they were in for a spell of rain, they were going to go to the pictures on Sunday, it was saveloys tonight in the mess. Once he'd filled the two pages it was, *Well, Nance, that's all the news for now, I'll say cheerio.* She treasured that connection across the years and wrote back with the same small news. Family was precious, a bond like no other, even if you didn't have much to talk about.

She was longing for Frank. Something had happened in that ragged growing-up. They'd lost touch with each other. If he came back she was going to find him again, the brother who'd been like an extension of herself, crouching in the cubby at Rothsay. Stay alive, Frank, she urged him in her mind. Just keep going, whatever it takes. She imagined what she'd say when they met again. Frank, she'd say, how did we drift apart? Let's start again and be a proper brother and sister again.

Reading the paper one day, she saw the headline 'Grave Shortage of Rubber'. All the rubber had come from the part of the world where Frank was. Perhaps at this very moment he was looking at a rubber tree and thinking that there must be a shortage back home, and for a piercing instant she felt joined to him across the miles. *Frank. Oh, Frank!*

Ken had made himself the shop steward at the *Ville d'Amiens* and was always trying to get the men out on strike. He was surprised and disappointed when none of them even showed up at the meetings. Nance thought, They're on a good wicket with all that *make a show* business, they're not going to spoil it. She was starting to see that while Ken was an intelligent man, he understood less than the most ignorant worker. She tried to tell him, but he dismissed her comments. The workers might be bought off for a while, he said, but they'd rise up when the time was right. With the right leadership.

One day he got home early. They've given me my money, he said. They could see I was making headway with the men. I was too dangerous for them. He regarded being sacked as a badge of honour. What a survivor he is, she thought. Everything turned to good account.

Before Manpower could get him, the comrades organised a course at Tech for him to become a Dilutee Fitter and Turner. The Dilutee part meant he wouldn't be a proper tradesman but good enough to be a wartime stand-in. He got his certificate and landed a job at a place called Morris Hearses, except that with the war on people were economising on hearses and the company was making trailers for the army instead. Ken was shop steward there too. Came home in high indignation about the primitive dunnies, a rough plank laid across a row of pans. Full of splinters, Nance! He was agitating for a fight with the boss. It could be a flashpoint, he said, and tried to call the men out on strike. But again nobody turned up to the meeting and again Ken was given his notice.

Then he got what he called a *gem of a job* over at Commonwealth Aircraft, where they were tooling up to make jet engines.

But isn't that war work, Ken? Nance asked.

No, Nance, he said, we're making the tools, not the engines.

She opened her mouth to say, That's splitting hairs!

He got in first. The Revolution takes the long view, Nance, he said.

Again he became shop steward, and again the dunnies were the issue. This time the problem was that they were so comfortable that the men were taking the racing pages in there for an hour at a time. The boss was threatening to dock their pay.

Fair enough, isn't it? Nance said. If it was my business, I wouldn't want to pay people to sit on the dunny reading the paper.

He was unruffled. It's a question of the historical moment, Nance, he said. Seeing it and seizing it.

But she started to feel some extra preoccupation in him, some extra withdrawal into his own thoughts, and braced herself for another story of his triumphant dismissal. Or was it that this time the Revolution really would start, right now, ignited by the dunnies at Commonwealth Aircraft?

Instead it was Ken coming home a month later from a Trotsky meeting with a look she'd never seen before. I'm out of it, Nance, he said.

She didn't know what he meant. Was he leaving her?

The Trotskyites, he said, impatiently, as if there could be no other reason for anything. Jim's left, Laurie's left. John always said it was a fantasy and he was right.

A fantasy, Nance said. But Trotsky...

Oh, Trotsky had some good ideas, he said. No doubt about that. But I've been there, I know. There's no international working class waiting for the Terminal Crisis. Just a lot of blokes diddling the system.

He was going back to his father's legal practice. His father wasn't well, couldn't manage the work any more.

I'm afraid the Fourth International, all six of them, will have to get along without me, he said.

She listened for the bitterness, the grief of someone whose dream had died. There was none. What an amazing man! Already it was a joke for him. He'd gone in one direction when it had looked right, and when those men he admired urged him to it. Now they'd moved on in a different direction and he was moving on with them. It was good to have an open mind and be willing to change your views. Still, wouldn't you expect a little more mourning?

Dolly wrote to say she had a job at the Repat Hospital at Concord but they couldn't give her a room, so she'd be stopping along with Nance and Ken for a time. Nance's first impulse was No! She told over to herself all the terrible things her mother had done to her. Sent her away at eight years old to live with people she'd never met. Farmed her out to the Medways. Oh, that woodheap and the longing to be an orphan! The scorn of *Oh, you children! You children don't matter!* If she'd had a proper childhood, been properly loved, she knew she'd have been able to refuse her mother. As it was, she couldn't. I'm trying to buy her love, she thought. If you don't get that love when you're a child, you're going to spend the rest of your life looking for it.

Ken didn't mind one way or the other, and she appreciated that. Many another man might have refused to have his querulous mother-in-law living with them. Over dinner Nance looked at them in amazement: her husband, the privileged Strathfield professional, and her mother, the rough country woman who called the Hawkesbury the Oxborough. Dolly would come back from a chest X-ray at the hospital and say, I had the rays but they weren't any good, I didn't feel the heat of them. Ken would listen politely and say, Really. Is that so. My word. With Nance later he enjoyed going over it again. *I didn't feel the heat of them!* Nance laughed along with him. It wasn't nice to laugh at your mother, but how good it was to have Ken warm and full of his old humour. Relief, too, came out of making the tyrant small.

Nance had got to know the pharmacist at the Ashfield Pharmacy. He'd gone through a few years ahead of her and remembered Charlie Gledhill. Oh, Charlie! he said. Now there was a character.

If you ever need anyone, Mr Felton, she said. You know, as a stopgap. My mother lives with us, she could look after the baby as long as it wasn't for too long.

Mr Felton looked surprised but not more than she was herself. It had flicked through her mind once or twice that she could do a bit of casual work. Hearing herself say it, almost on impulse, she wondered at the other Nance inside the one she knew.

Mr Felton was keen. With so many pharmacists away fighting, everyone was short-handed. What about next week, Mrs Gee, he said. Say, Thursday and Friday?

Walking home she thought, What have I got myself into? Explaining to Ken, squaring it with Dolly, and hadn't she always said she hated pharmacy? But it would only be a couple of days here and there. The money would make a big difference. And if she was truthful, the idea of being out in the world again—just now and then—was exciting. Christopher was a year old and she'd been with him night and day for that year. She'd loved every minute. But while she was a mother, she was also a person. Dolly wasn't a warm grandma, but Christopher would be safe with her. Soon enough Dolly would take off again, and the chance to make a few pounds would go with her.

Ken had made good money as a worker. There'd been all sorts of perks with overtime and tool allowances. At his father's practice he made much less. He didn't have the knack of buttering up the old folk who came in to have a look at their will and a long yarn about nothing much. They still asked for old Mr Gee, not the new Mr Gee who was a bit too brisk. When money did come in you never knew how long you'd have to make it last. Clients might pay their account straight away, or not for months.

She made light of her plan to Ken, pretended she was missing the pharmacy work, needed to keep her hand in. You had to save a man's pride, she thought. It turned out that his pride didn't need protecting. As long as Nance was home at both ends of the day, what she did in between wasn't his concern.

Leaving Christopher on the first morning was agonising. His face contorted with entreaty, his eyes locked on hers, his arms stretched out pathetically. She got to the end of the street and had to turn back, crept along the side path and there he was out the back with Dolly, pushing his wagon about on the grass. His cheeks were still shiny with tears but all his new teeth were showing in a smile at his own cleverness.

She slipped back into the work as if she'd never stopped: taking the script and seeing at a glance what the doctor wanted, going to the bottles to mix up the stuff, smiling at the customers and listening to them complain about their rheumatism. She loved the bustle of the shop, the way you had to be thinking all the time, because everyone who came in had a different problem. Catching sight of herself in the weighing-machine mirror, pink-cheeked with pleasure after seeing off someone else singing her praises, she amazed herself. She'd always hated pharmacy. So why was she seeing the face of a happy woman in the little circle of mirror?

Impressive, Mr Felton said, and smiled warmly into her eyes. She could see he liked her. She wasn't interested, but, oh, it felt good to have a man look at you admiringly.

Mrs Gee, you're an impressive woman, he said. She didn't get much of that at home.

Two months later Dolly announced she was going to Walgett to help in the pub that Auntie Rose had leased there. Walgett was a long way away, right out in the west of the state. Nance waved her off with no regrets. The work had been energising, and not too much of it, a few days here and there. She'd proved that she could still work, and enjoy it. What should come next had gradually made itself clear to her. She didn't want Christopher to be an only child. It was time to make sure he had a brother or sister. That bond she had with Max and especially with Frank was precious. No one should go through life without something like it.

She was surprised that Ken readily agreed. It made her think that he must really love Christopher in his own way. He can't show the feelings, she decided, but he must have them. And the reality was that whether they had one child or two wasn't going to make any difference to him. His life would still be elsewhere. She'd be the one looking after the new child, as she'd been the one doing everything for Christopher.

The new baby was due around Christmas 1943. The pains started after they'd come home from Christmas lunch at the Gees'. Dolly had come to stay with them again, just till the baby was born, so Nance put Christopher to bed, and she and Ken started walking to the little hospital round the corner where she was booked in. It was only a few blocks but she realised she was cutting it fine. The pains came every minute or so, making her stop and lean against someone's fence until they passed. Cars rushed along and whirled the grit up in their wake, the pain came on her in a huge unfriendly gripe. She turned to Ken but he was standing apart from her, looking off up the road. The pain was taking the words away but she wanted to shout, Put your arm around me! Take my hand, anything, but be a human being!

He was embarrassed, she understood that. He was frightened too. The baby might come there and then on the footpath on King Street, Ashfield, and he'd have to do something that he didn't know how to do. But she was frightened too, and what sort of person could turn aside at such a time?

They got to the hospital in time and Stephen was born on Boxing Day. Christopher had been a restless baby, whereas Stephen lay in her arms watching her, thoughtful and serene. What a humbling mystery it was, the way the sperm and the egg from the same couple could produce two such different new humans. You had to do your best for whatever person nature presented you with. But you weren't completely responsible for the person the baby grew into, because that person was there from the beginning.

By the time Stephen was six months old Nance had come to accept that Ken didn't love her. Something had shifted in her the night he'd stood aside on the way to the hospital and nothing had happened since then to shift it back.

He'd never told her he loved her, not once in three years of marriage. *Admire* and *esteem* was as close as he'd ever got. The wit and charm were still there, and the warm beam of it was still directed at others. But not to her.

Sometimes he was so distant she thought there must be another woman. She asked him one day but he seemed astonished. Astonished, or a wonderful actor? It was beneath her dignity to spy. Another woman would only bring a literal dimension to what was true in spirit: she couldn't touch any true emotion in him.

In anger sometimes she wondered if he'd only married her because she was a pharmacist and could earn money. Or because all his friends were getting married. He liked the idea of her, she thought, rather than the reality of the person she was.

At other times she blamed herself. Her face was too big, her hair was too thin, her eyes were too small. She wasn't feminine enough. She was too bossy, too much of a know-all, she argued too much.

In the end, though, she always returned to the same truth: she could only be the person she was. She'd thought that would be enough, and he must have thought so too. If that was turning out to be wrong, no one was to blame. He'd never pretended, never promised anything. She was the one who'd pretended. She'd told herself that he wasn't loving towards her only because he didn't know how to be, that his cold upbringing had made him frightened of showing feelings. Now she was prepared to face the facts: needing to be loved, she'd invented a love in him that he didn't feel. She had to face something else, too: she still loved him, even though the cloth of her love had been rubbed into holes by his indifference.

She thought again about leaving but again she drew back. It was too drastic to deprive the boys of their father. From her own life she knew that children without a proper home life had the feeling they were second-class citizens. Always apologising about something. She thought it was why she'd picked the wrong man: she hadn't had enough experience of love. She didn't want to do that to her children. It was better to sacrifice one generation and break the cycle of unhappy unsettled adults having unhappy unsettled children. And, if you did that, you had to do it with your whole heart. Not do what her mother had done: stay, but taint all the lives around you with your unhappiness. Not being loved was a bleak and chronic pain like a toothache. But admitting and even accepting it let you become a person again. Not being loved didn't have to stop you. You had to get on and live your life around that fact.

There were times, too, when the marriage was companionable. A book or a film could set the two of them off on a conversation, let them take pleasure in engaging with each other's minds. Sometimes, Nance felt a good old argument about a film was the best part of their marriage. If I can't have love, she thought, I'm willing to settle for a companion.

Above all, the children made sense of everything. She might not be happy, but nature didn't care about happiness. It only cared about putting the right egg together with the right sperm. She and Ken had come together thinking it was because they liked each other, but something more primitive was at work, something that allowed each to recognise the other as good mating material. All those frogs puffing out their throats, bowerbirds collecting blue things, pigeons strutting and bobbing: it was all right to admit that this particular breeding pair wasn't so far removed from them.

THIRTEEN

AS CHRISTOPHER got older there were problems with Mrs MacFadyean, the landlady in the other half of the house. She'd thump on the wall and pass Nance on the side path with a glare. *Mrs Gee, that child is uncontrollable.* It didn't seem to Nance that Christopher was doing anything worse than a normal three-year-old could be expected to do. He made a bit of noise sometimes, and he'd pulled up one of her salvias. She shushed him as much as she could, and replaced the salvia. After Stephen was born Mrs MacFadyean was even crankier. Some mothers shouldn't even have one child let alone two to run wild, she told the woman over the fence, plenty loud enough. Nance wanted to say, They're lively clever children, Mrs MacFadyean, do you wish yours were lively and clever too?

Every Saturday she went through the classifieds but nothing for rent was ever right for them. People wanted a tidy single woman or a quiet business couple. Landlords could pick and choose because there'd been no new housing built for four years, and people were flooding into Sydney for the war work. She rang about one place, just on the off-chance. The woman sounded friendly. And what about a child? Nance asked. She thought she'd better not say there were two. On no account, the woman said. No children.

At last, one Saturday in June 1944, she saw *Nicely furnished cottage to let, close to bus, Wishart, Crescent Road, Mona Vale*. Mona Vale was north of the city, on the coast, the suburb before Newport, where Dolly had run Beach House when Nance was six. It was a long way out, but there was a bus. Back then, Bert had come from the grocery shop on a Friday night by bus. He'd told her that when it got to Bushranger's Hill it had to turn around and go up backwards because the hill was so steep. It was one of those little things you remembered from your childhood but now she wondered, Had he been fooling her? The memory brought back the smell of salt in the air, the rumble of the surf, the way the afternoon nor'easter made Pittwater roughen and sparkle.

Ken frowned down at the newspaper. She watched his face, that surface she knew so well, that showed so little. What calculation was going on in his mind that would end in a yes or a no?

There'll be a bus in twenty minutes, he said. Think we can make it?

When they got to the place in Crescent Road they

were shocked, there must have been forty people milling about on the front lawn. Mr Wishart was frowning and laughing at the same time. So many! he kept exclaiming. So many people! Nance could see he had no idea how to play God for one lucky person. He was some kind of Continental, with his hair combed straight back the way they did, and his head a square sort of shape. You could hear the accent but his English was all right. Poor man, he was overwhelmed.

Ken went over to talk to him. He pointed at Nance standing with the boys and she smiled. Mr Wishart smiled back and she saw the glint of gold in a tooth.

No good, Ken said when he joined her again. All these people. We weren't even the first.

He took Christopher by the hand and turned away. Oh, you Strathfield types, she thought. Going by the rules and giving up at the first hurdle! She rammed the pram up the bumpy grass, good thing Stephen was such a patient baby, because he was being bounced around like a cabbage in a basket.

Ah, Mr Wishart, she called, and he came down the steps smiling.

Call me Louis, dear, he said.

We've got a place, she said. It's only that the landlady doesn't like the children. But if you gave us your place, we could give someone ours. Then two people would be happy, not just one.

She knew all the other people must have a place too, unless they were living in caves. But it gave Louis what he needed, a reason to pick one person and not another. It was settled, and what came next should have been her handing over a deposit.

Oh, we came without any money, she cried. She was starting to panic. She'd been so clever but now she'd lose the place! I'll leave you my coat, she said. Look, it's good wool, I'll leave you that.

She was taking it off, but Louis stopped her and pulled the coat back up her arm. Took his time settling the collar. She felt his hand against her hair.

No need for that, dear, he said. If a man can't trust a woman, what's life worth?

The house in Crescent Road was a little weatherboard place, dunny out the back, the only hot water the chip heater in the bathroom, singing clouds of mosquitoes as soon as the sun slid down behind the ridge. But it was paradise after the gritty streets of Ashfield. She loved being out among trees, each one as individual as a person, the kookaburras lined up along a branch watching you, and that holiday feel of salt in the air. She never tired of the way the light moved over the water and the bush, the big sky with its endless drama of clouds and sunsets.

Mona Vale was mostly market gardens and poultry farms. The milkman still used a horse and cart to deliver. His name was Homer but he was no bard, only an ignorant man who called the Hawkesbury the Oxborough the way Dolly did. You could get extra butter from him, black market, but Nance stayed on the straight and narrow because of Frank. Half a pound of under-the-counter butter now and then wasn't going to make any difference to the war effort, but it would be like taunting the gods.

It was an inconvenient sort of place. There was a grocery shop within walking distance, but for everything else you had to get the bus. If you went north to Newport there was a butcher, and Buford's where they ran a flag up when the ice had arrived from the ice-works, and the barber who gave you a penny back if he nicked your ear. South, in the village of Mona Vale, there were a few more shops, but the nearest pharmacy was all the way down at Narrabeen. She got to know Mr Quinn, the pharmacist there. He was older than she was but they'd had some of the same instructors at university. He didn't remember Charlie Gledhill, but he knew the Enmore Pharmacy. Every time she went into the shop he'd say, Fancy a job then, Mrs Gee? They'd have a laugh, Nance with a child on each hand.

It took Ken over an hour on buses to get to his father's office in Auburn. Now and then he stayed in town overnight, with his parents, he said, or with Laurie or Jim. She didn't let herself wonder. In the late afternoon she'd take the boys to meet him at the bus stop, the same way her mother had taken her and her brothers to meet their father on a Friday afternoon. The boys would run to Ken and he'd swing them up into his arms. Seeing the three of them together, she knew she was right to stay.

He never complained about the long bus ride. In fact she thought it was the remoteness of Mona Vale, its foreign feeling, that freed something in him. No one in the Strathfield house would have dreamed of picking up a hammer or getting their hands dirty growing vegetables, but at Mona Vale he took the skills he'd learned as a dilutee tradesman and made them into the pleasure of his free time. He designed a chook house, drawing with his thick builder's pencil on the back of an envelope. The idea was to give it wheels so you could push it to a new piece of ground every so often. Nance thought it would be too heavy to move. She told herself to hold her tongue. Ken let the boys help, showing them how to use the bit and brace, sympathising when they missed with the hammer.

The chook house looked magnificent but it sank to the axles in the soft ground as she'd thought it would. Untroubled, Ken found another envelope and started to sketch another idea.

That's the difference between us, she thought. For me, a project is about making something work. For Ken, it's the pleasure of nutting out the physics of it. The chook house was like Trotsky's revolution: a lovely theory that fell apart in the real world.

One night he came home driving a strange-looking car with a square cabin at the front with space for two people and tapering away to a point at the back. He boasted about what a bargain it had been and what a good car it was. It's an Essex Super Six, Nance! A sports car!

But the boys, Ken, she said. Where are they going to go?

Oh, I'll cut them a dicky seat in the back, he said.

She thought he was joking and walked off so he wouldn't see how cranky she was. What was the use, the money was spent now. But at the weekend he got to work with the cold chisel and the hacksaw and finally had a hole big enough to slip in a wooden box for a seat. It looked strange but she had to admit it worked. The boys thought it was wonderful, squashed in there with the slipstream making their hair stand on end.

As Ken tinkered away with his projects she'd hear him singing softly, *The people's flag is deepest red*, or murmuring to himself. It was like hearing two old friends having a conversation. She was coming to see that he was most at ease on his own. Something in him had been driven underground by that family life where he'd always been the odd man out.

He taught her to drive. He was a good teacher, methodical and patient. It didn't seem hard, the co-ordination on the clutch no more complicated than working the Singer. The Essex had been adapted to run on kerosene because of petrol rationing and it stalled easily. You had to get out, fold the bonnet back and prime the carby. That wasn't as hard as you might think, once you were shown. Give credit where it's due, she thought, Ken isn't one of those men who keeps a wife helpless.

When she went to do the driving test she put the boys in the dicky seat, but Stephen was upset about something and couldn't stop crying. The policeman was a kindly older man. Oh, give me the little one, he said, so Stephen perched on his knee while she did the test. People complain about women drivers, the policeman said, signing the certificate. Far as I'm concerned they're worth a dozen show-off men. Best of luck, Mrs Gee.

They got to know Louis Wishart well. He was renting them the cottage because his wife had gone off with another man and he wanted to keep things going in case she came back. He was German, he'd jumped ship twenty years before. Now he lived in a little place across the road from the cottage on a couple of acres he owned, and grew tomatoes in hothouses.

He was cheerful and friendly, liked a laugh, kept them supplied with tomatoes. Taught Christopher and Stephen some German swear words and thought it was a great joke to hear them shouting *Himmel donnerwetter!* It's only like damn and blast, Nance, he said. Nothing bad, I promise.

Louis' place had no hot water, so he'd knock on their door on a Saturday afternoon, have a bath and spruce himself up ready for a night at the Newport Arms. He was a dapper fellow, liked to wear a suit and tie even at the Arms. It was the Continental way, Nance thought. She'd be aware of him lying in the water, imagined him soaping the hair on his chest. She'd hear when he pulled out the plug and sluiced down the bath. The room was always immaculate after he'd used it.

He'd come out washed, shaved and in his suit, and have a beer with Nance and Ken. He was a communist, so he and Ken had plenty to talk about. Ken enjoyed showing off how much more he knew about Marx than Louis did. Loved to prove him wrong on some point of theory. Louis didn't argue, just smiled and nodded. When he told them about how terrible things had been in the Germany he'd left, so much worse than it had ever been in Australia, she saw that, for him, communism was a belief too deep to need logic. She understood that. Ken could always win an argument, but that didn't mean he was always right.

There were evenings when she felt Louis was in no hurry to get away. They'd have the wireless playing and, when dance music came on, Louis would stand up, click his heels and put out his hand to Nance. At the end of the dance he'd take her to Ken and Ken would get up and dance too. How dancing reveals a person, she thought. Ken held her formally, used his hands and elbows to lead. Not as good as Astaire, but in the same elegant mathematical style. Louis gathered her in, used his whole body to show her what he had in mind, smiled comfortably as he danced.

He told them one evening that, when the war started, he'd got a grilling from Special Branch. They thought he was a Nazi because he went to the German club in the city. I told them I was only going there for the girls, he said, but they didn't believe me. So I did the foxtrot for them in their office. My word, that did it.

They knew a Nazi could never dance like that!

So do all German men dance as well as you do, Louis? Nance asked.

He looked affronted. Certainly not, he said. Most German men dance like sausages. In a bun. With sauerkraut and mustard!

And you, Louis, she said, what do you dance like?

A glass of champagne, he said. He said it the French way, a soft flourish of a word. Plenty of bubbles and love, and no headache in the morning.

Homer told them that nearby Waterview Street was called the Mad Half Mile because all the people who lived there were pinkos and artists. It turned out that Ken and Nance knew one of those pinkos, Guido Baracchi. He'd been in the party with Ken, had been Comrade Barker. Nance had never much cared for him, in spite of his courtly European manners, but she liked his wife Ula. She'd been a nurse, was a sensible clever woman. She had a little girl from a husband she'd left when she went off with Guido. *A perfectly nice man*, Ula called that abandoned husband, and Nance thought she heard the tone of regret.

Guido and Ula were hospitable and invited Ken and Nance to meet the other Mad Half Mile people. Arthur Murch was a painter. He'd brought along a picture he'd done of his wife. Nance thought it was a very good painting, but she wondered how his wife could be so calm with everyone looking at her naked up on the wall. She just said, Look, hasn't Arthur given me a nice bosom? Better than my flea bites! Arthur had trained as an engineer but painting was his passion.

His wife's name was Ria. When she introduced herself to Nance she put out her hand to shake, like a man. I'm Ria, she said. Not diarrhoea, not gonorrhoea, just Ria. Until her children were born Ria had worked for one of the city papers as a journalist. Oh, Ria was the breadwinner, Arthur said proudly. And will be again, unless someone decides I'm Michelangelo! That was new to Nance: not the idea of the woman as breadwinner, but the man not being ashamed of it.

Weaver Hawkins was a painter too, but apparently quite famous and, unlike Arthur, he made a living from his art. He was a modest quiet man with something wrong with his hands, he'd been wounded in the first war. He introduced himself and his wife Rene by saying, We are rationalists, socialists and nonconformists. He was English, had that crisp upper-class way of talking, but he and Rene wore funny drapy clothes and great clunky homemade sandals. Nonconformist. Did that just mean Methodist?

Nance was out of her depth. She'd never heard of Annie Besant or Henry Moore. But she liked these people. They never made her feel foolish. They were honest and straightforward and didn't care about doing things the way everyone else did them. She thought they had the right idea, living for their art, their beliefs and the pleasures of life. Her parents had put money-making at the centre of their lives because they didn't know anything else to put there, and where had it got them? An unhappy marriage, unhappy children, and then they'd lost the lot.

I suppose they all think of themselves as bohemians, Ken said on the way home, and he gave the word a mocking slant. That was what he'd have liked to be, she thought. Fearless and free-thinking. It was what the Trotsky time had been about. He loved to be the one running against the herd.

During the week she spent a lot of time with the women from the Mad Half Mile. They'd take their children swimming in the shallows at the end of Mona Vale Beach or wind down the track for a picnic at Bungan Beach. Nance watched to see how they did things, because she was making up motherhood as she went along. Her own childhood had given only the certainty that she didn't want to repeat what had been done to her. The other mothers weren't sure either. It was a bond, sharing the doubts and the dilemmas. Perhaps there was no right way, she decided. There were certainly wrong ways, and she'd had that. Still, children did survive. She had, after all.

Her two boys were so different in temperament— there were days when it seemed they'd never stop arguing, one provoking the other, the moment ending in tears and each saying the other did it. She never hit them, though her mother and father had hit her. But when she was at the end of her tether she heard her voice go like

Dolly's, the voice that had made her shrink as a child. She hated herself for it, but it worked. The boys' little faces closed, they looked at her sideways, fearfully, and for a while they stopped squabbling.

The other mothers were happy to let the afternoon drift past, chatting about nothing much, watching the breakers swell, bulge, break, run out into foam, then pull back and start all over again. Nance loved those times too, but there was always a gap between her and the others. As the women sat there, moving the umbrella to chase the shade, she'd start to feel restless. She wanted to be doing. She might start to think about the possum fence she was going to try to rig up to keep her lettuce safe—could she get some chicken wire from somewhere? Homer might know a farmer who had a bit out the back she could get cheap or swap for some eggs, but that mightn't work because everyone had eggs. Perhaps she could knit them a pair of socks. Not everyone knew how to turn a heel.

There wasn't much money around, and with the war on you couldn't buy things. But she enjoyed the problems. Like Ken, she loved kneading away at a difficulty, loved to have a project. The other mothers didn't seem to be driven in the same way. Was this the same dangerous restlessness that warped Dolly's life? Always looking for a way to make things better, and ending up making them worse?

Rene got appendicitis and had to be rushed to the hospital down at Manly. Weaver and Guido visited her together every day. Weaver couldn't drive and Guido had a Manpower job driving a Ve-Toy Biscuits delivery truck.

Nance wanted to do something for Rene, so she gave Weaver oranges from their tree to take to Rene in the hospital.

A few days later Weaver came round to their place with a painting he'd done of Bungan Beach.

A little thing to say thank you, Nance, for your kindness, he said. Rene was very appreciative. And so was I.

Nance was embarrassed. The painting was more than she deserved for a few oranges! She'd never owned a real painting before. Not just a painting, she thought: a work of art. She looked at it so closely she realised she'd never really looked at a painting before. Sometimes when Ken had been dealing with the hecklers in the Domain she'd wandered over to the Art Gallery, but nothing she'd seen there had anything to do with her life. This was different. Bungan Beach was one of the boys' favourite picnic spots, and she loved it too. She'd scramble down the rough track, through the scrappy windswept bushes, the boys running along ahead. She loved the place, but she'd never thought of it as something you'd paint a picture of. It wasn't Venice, or Paris, or any of the places the Art Gallery was full of.

Weaver had caught the exact feel of the beach she loved. With a thump of recognition she saw the track, the coarse golden sand. You could just about smell the salt. Yet it wasn't like a photo. Weaver had moved the track so it wound down the slope differently, had brought the headland closer. It was as if he'd seen past the surface to the essence of the place, some truth beyond the real. She felt as if she was seeing that familiar landscape for the first time.

If you looked closely you could see the white paper that Weaver had left to make the foam on the waves. The painting was a window onto Bungan Beach but it was also just coloured water. You could see how it had been done, and that showed you the mind of the man doing it. It was a picture of his thoughts as much as a picture of a landscape. She'd have liked to talk about it with him, but was shy of making a fool of herself. She didn't know the proper words for any of it. And you might not be supposed to notice the white paper.

Ken was bored at his father's practice. His father didn't believe in litigation, he said. It was un-British to quarrel, and to go to court was beneath a gentleman's dignity, so Ken did nothing but conveyancing and probate. I'm fed up with it, Nance, he announced. Never want to unravel the intricacies of another Old System title.

Some former Trotsky comrades offered him a position at their firm in the city. Sullivans didn't bother with Old System titles. They did litigation for the unions, mostly for industrial negligence. The way Ken explained it, you found someone with a bad back, then you got them to put in a claim for what he loved to call *the nello*.

Dolly wrote to say she had a peach of a job, attendant in the ladies' bathroom at the luxurious Australia Hotel in the city. She had to wear a little black uniform, very smart she said, with a dainty white apron and cap. At the end of each day she took home all the little cakes of once-used soaps and gave them to Nance when she came to see them. Soap was one thing Nance never had to buy.

Then Dolly was off work with bronchitis and when she went back they'd got someone else. She came to stay with Nance and Ken again. Nance had forgotten how hard her mother was to live with. She was full of complaints about how far Mona Vale was from everything. Found the pinkos of the Mad Half Mile shocking. Criticised her daughter for the way she was spoiling the boys. Nance, you're making a rod for your own back, she said, and sounded pleased. She complained that she wasn't getting her fair share of the tea ration, the butter ration. Nance started to keep her mother's rations separate and Dolly soon saw how careful you had to be and went back to putting her coupons in with everyone else's.

Still, there were times during the day when mother and daughter would have a cup of tea in the kitchen and talk about old times. Dolly loved to remember the Cally at Tamworth. She'd go through it room by room, the firedogs in the guests' lounge, people were always wanting to buy them, the big tinted photos of Monte Carlo with the gilt frames—those frames alone worth twenty pounds, Nance!—and the great mahogany dining table with the four extra leaves and the spoon-backed cedar chairs. Florence Austral had sung for them, Isador Goodman had admired the tone of the piano. Singing for their supper, Dolly said, and laughed till the coughing stopped her.

She never said, I'm sorry. But for Nance it was enough to have her mother beside her with that soft look on her face. Their memories were like coins they passed to each other, warm from one hand into the other.

AT the Mad Half Mile, 1946. Dolly and Christopher third from left, Ken holding Stephen. 'It was quite a little community down at Mona Vale. It was only a little area and I think everybody knew everybody else's business. I didn't realise it at the time, but looking back I think they probably did.'

BUNGAN Beach, painted by Weaver Hawkins, 1946.

DOLLY, 1947. 'When I started the pharmacy, Mum promised to stay. She'd always be there, look after the children, do everything. But I hardly had the pharmacy going a few months when she said, Oh no, I can't stay here!'

NANCE with Stephen, Christopher and neighbours, and the longed-for bricks, 1947.

'CLEM Seale lived nearby—he was an artist on one of the papers and did a pen and ink drawing of the house—I think he only charged something like ten pounds, and that reluctantly.'

WIFE HELPS TO BUILD HOME

Wife of Sydney solicitor Kenneth Gee is helping him to build their own home at Mona Vale.

Solicitor stops arguing, builds

Tired of arguing with builders over prices, city solicitor Kenneth Gee is saving £600 by building his own home at Mona Vale with the help of his wife and two children.

He says families wanting houses should form groups in their districts and co-operate in building them.

"Builders don't seem interested in getting the work done, and their prices are far too high," he said.

"I bought three books — one on bricklaying, one about carpentering and a third on building practice.

"They cost me 17/- and by studying them from cover to cover, I got enough knowledge to begin building."

Gee started building in January, has laid the brick foundations and framework.

He has promised his son, Christopher that the family will move into the weather-board cottage on his birthday in August.

His only building equipment is a trowel, plum bob, hammer, floor cramp, a saw and a spanner.

"My wife loves all the brickwork and is helping with the flooring.

"Through the week, she spends her spare time driving nails into the floor boards.

"The house has two bedrooms, a large lounge, kitchen, laundry and bathroom.

"I've left plenty of room for expansion, and will start building another room as soon as we move in."

The original plan for Gee's house was drawn up by his architect brother.

THE *Sun* newspaper, 1947. 'They took a photo of me on the roof—they wanted me to show that all you had to do was nail it. They didn't say how hard the nailing was, though!'
Reproduced courtesy of the State Library of New South Wales.

KEN, Nance, Stephen and Christopher on the verandah of the new house, 1948.

BABY Kate with her brothers.

KEN, 1949.

NANCE with her assistant in the Balgowlah pharmacy, 1954.

NANCE, on left,
with a friend in
the city, 1958.

ULURU, 1959. Nance on right, Bill Harney centre.

UNIVERSITÉ DE PARIS

COURS DE CIVILISATION FRANÇAISE
À LA SORBONNE

SEMESTRE D'HIVER 1965-1966

INSCRIPTION TOTALE
(férences et cours pratique)

Madame GEE Nance

Nationalité australienne

Adresse 18 rue de Constantinople (8°)

Carte délivrée le 14 décembre 1965

ription est définitive. Aucun remboursement n'est accordé.

1965: Nance's first travel beyond Australia, aged fifty-three.

BA (Hons), University of Sydney, 1968.

NANCE aged eighty-four.

FOURTEEN

ONE DAY in 1945 Louis came to them and said he was planning to sell off part of his land. Did they want to buy it?

Nance had brought her savings into the marriage, a hundred and fifty pounds. Ken had about the same. Buying the land would clean them out. But buying and selling, buying and selling: she'd grown up with the power of capital to change lives. She feared Ken might still be enough under the sway of Trotsky to resist, but he was ahead of her with all the arguments. Rent was dead money, Louis' land was a beautiful block and big enough that they could subdivide later if they wanted to.

On the title deed Nance and Ken were listed as joint owners. Ken was *Kenneth Grenville Gee, Solicitor*. She was *Nance Isobel Gee, his wife*. It was only a piece of paper no one would ever see again, but she wished she'd made the solicitor change it. *Nance Isobel Gee, Pharmacist*.

Signing the papers, she could feel her heart going too fast. She kept thinking of her father standing in the doorway of the Cally the day they'd left for Mittagong. Nothing could go wrong, and then it did. She and Ken had spent all they had and they didn't even have a house, only an acre of land with a tumbledown hothouse, a grove of bananas and a great glossy bank of Monstera deliciosa. He was making better money at Sullivans than he had at his father's, but it would take years to save enough for even a modest place.

At Narrabeen, Mr Quinn said as usual, Don't suppose you'd like a job, Mrs Gee?

This time she didn't laugh. She said, What would I do with the boys, Mr Quinn? She saw his surprise, looking from her eyes to her mouth and back again to see if she was joking.

It was nothing as deliberate as a decision. She had no idea what she'd do with the boys. But she knew she was going to take the job.

My mother's with us, she said. What was she doing thinking out loud with this man? The only thing is, she's not reliable. And Christopher's due to start school next year.

Well, I tell you what, Mr Quinn said, there's a little school round the corner. Takes them nearly from babies. Lakeside, Lake View, some name like that. Children running around naked, people call it the Babies' Brothel!

Lakehouse School had a sign on the gate but it was

an ordinary house. A woman called Guyda showed her around. It wasn't like any school she'd ever seen. There were two big sunny classrooms. No blackboards, no rows of desks, just low tables. No stiff-faced children chanting the seven-times tables, and no one pouncing on them to spell *indeed*. No one running around naked, either. At one table a little girl doing a drawing had her head on one side and her tongue out the corner of her mouth. By the window three boys were laying coloured wooden blocks in patterns. A couple of children were sprawled on big pillows, reading. Out on the verandah a boy was bossing some others around, putting on a play. That's our Jack, Guyda said fondly. He's going to be an actor, you know.

Guyda told her the philosophy of the school: a school should fit the child, not the other way around. Nance thought, That's all very well, but what about reading and arithmetic? Guyda knew what she was thinking. I assure you, Mrs Gee, by the time the children leave here they can all read and write and do sums. She pointed to the boys with the coloured blocks. We don't call it arithmetic, Mrs Gee, but that's what it is.

The school should fit the child. She thought of her own childhood freedom, running around the paddocks at Rothsay with Frank, dreaming her way through the trees. Once in their lifetime, a person should have that kind of freedom.

Lakehouse School took children from as young as three, boarders as well as day pupils. Guyda said she'd take both boys, even though Stephen was not quite three.

For a little extra, they could stay on after school with the boarders until Nance finished work.

It was an outrageous sort of school. But she thought, I've broken away from my own background. Got more education than anyone else in the family and married a man from a different world. Why not think differently about what a school could be?

Ken didn't take much persuading that working at Quinn's was a good idea. He was as keen as she was to get the money for the house. He didn't ask what arrangements she was planning to make for the boys. When she told him about Lakehouse School he did no more than nod. The children were her concern.

Dolly saw a place for herself in the new set-up. Promised to keep the house clean and tidy and get the tea ready of an evening. It would be a big help, Nance agreed. It was the one good side to her mother's restlessness, she thought: Dolly had never been frightened of hard work. She was always fired up at the prospect of something new, something better.

When Nance left the boys at Lakehouse School on the first day, Stephen was already playing with a board criss-crossed with shoelaces and Christopher had found a box of Meccano. They hardly looked up to say goodbye. Still, her heart was pinched at leaving them. She should be the one teaching them to read and kissing them better when they fell over. She was doing what her own mother had done—sending them off, too young.

It wasn't much fun being in the shop with Mr Quinn.

He was glad to have her there, but really he thought a mother shouldn't be working. She'd catch him watching her, this woman whose husband couldn't keep her.

The money started to build up in the bank, but she was impatient at how slowly the numbers got bigger. Nance knew the arithmetic of pharmacy as well as the chemistry of it. She knew what Mr Quinn paid in rent and what he paid her. She knew the mark-up on every bottle of aspirin. The profit he made was an easy sum to do. Marx was right: you'd never get rich on a wage.

It was such a mad idea that the first time it came to her she snuffed it out. It came back rich with detail. What would it be like to have her own pharmacy? Work for herself and keep the profit?

She supposed it was impossible. The mothers of young children might go out to work, though that was rare. But she couldn't think of any who had their own business. If she started up her own pharmacy, she'd be a one-off. Still, she woke up with it in her mind every morning.

She brought it up one night over dinner. There'd be an opening for a pharmacy in Newport, she said. I could start one, you know. Ken glanced at her, his face the careful blank of lawyer's caution.

On your own, he said. A pharmacy.

Yes, Ken, she said. She stopped herself from saying, Otherwise the boys will be grown up before we get enough for a house. Parted her lips in the silence to let the unspoken words evaporate.

A small place, she said. Start in a small way.

But Dolly already had the shop up and running. Oh yes, Nance, she said. Nothing closer than Quinn's, and all those people giving themselves headaches on the beach, you'll make a fortune on the Aspros alone!

Her mother's enthusiasm almost made Nance doubt. Would this be another perfect scheme that would turn sour?

After the reflex caution, Ken threw himself into the idea. Went through the numbers with her, and wondered if there was any chance the bank would extend a line of credit if he pretended it was for him. You'd have to have a place near the bus stop, and would she need an assistant or should she get an apprentice? The only thing he didn't think of was the biggest one: how to make sure the boys would be all right.

She thought it could work, though she'd never seen it done. She'd drive the boys to school in the morning and drive back to open the shop. Then in the afternoon she'd close up a bit early to drive back down to Narrabeen to pick them up.

All of it was a risk. Dolly promised hand on heart that she'd stay, but she wasn't reliable. It would be a lot of driving. It would be touch-and-go at the start, paying out rent and building up a business from scratch. But marrying Ken had been a risk. Moving to Mona Vale had been a risk. Putting everything they had into the land had been a risk. Imagine if I stay behind the counter at Quinn's, she thought, putting a few pounds away every week.

Yes, we'd be safe, but we'd only be half alive. Sometimes in life you have to jump.

The simplest thing nearly stopped her before she even started: there were no shops to rent in Newport. There was a cottage next to the grocery, but it was for sale, not rent. However, word had got around the Mad Half Mile, Nance Gee was going to start a pharmacy. Ula came to her one day: would Nance be interested in a partner? She had some money from before she'd married Guido and could buy the cottage. Nance would have the pharmacy in one room and Ula would run a home-nursing business from the other.

Nance felt her face taking on Ken's lawyerly blank. It was surely too good to be true. So Ula told her the full story. She wanted to make a life of her own, because Guido's eye was roving again. He'd charmed her away from her *perfectly nice* husband with a lovely old poem, she said. Gone down on one knee, recited it with tears in his eyes. Ula knew he had his eye on someone else now, because he'd been hunting around the house for the book with the poem in it.

Nance told Mr Quinn. Oh yes, Mrs Gee, he said. Your own place. Certainly. She'd come to hate the way he stood at the door of the shop, looking out and humming with a little pleased smile on his face. If ever she doubted, that look was a goad. She would not be stopped.

There were endless delays with permissions. You had to get a *Licence to Purchase Poison*, a *Certificate of*

Compliance for how you stored the poisons, a *Certificate of Inspection* that a man had come and approved of the locks on the dispensary. Nance was supposed to produce the piece of paper she'd been given on the day she was registered as a pharmacist. In all the moves it had gone missing, so she had to go to the university and arrange to get a duplicate, and no one was going to hurry about it. There were days when she felt like Columbus, sure of the Indies when everyone thought he'd fall off the edge of the earth. Or Cortez. *All his men / Looked at each other with a wild surmise.* That was the look she wanted to see on Mr Quinn's face.

At last the news came that they'd all been longing to hear: on the second of September 1945 the Japanese surrendered. Nance came home from Quinn's to find Dolly rushing off a letter to Frank. She glanced over her mother's shoulder. *My dearest son, at last you are free, I thank Almighty God for your deliverance.* It was a surprise to Nance that her mother was thinking in terms of Almighty God. God had never seemed any part of Dolly's life. But no one knew that Nance had lit that prayerful candle for Frank. She thought, What mysteries we all are to each other.

He'd come and stay with them. The boys could go into the sleepout and Frank would have their room. She'd have to fatten him up, cosset him. She'd sit with him and talk. Remember the cubby at Rothsay? How the sun slanted in, how the dust was as fine as talcum powder, how it was so quiet you could hear the river running over the stones way down at the end of the paddock?

She was coming out of Quinn's a few weeks later, putting her coat on, and almost brushed past Ken waiting outside. Nance, he said. She was startled, looked at him as if he was a stranger.

I've got very bad news, Nance, he said. Frank is dead. No, she said. No, no.

The telegram came today, he said. I'm sorry, Nance. But he didn't put his arms around her, and that was what she needed, to be held tight, because otherwise everything inside her was going to float off out into the great hostile world that had taken Frank away. Then there was nothing but the bleak drive home, Ken silent beside her. Even before she went into the house she could hear Dolly shouting and crying as if someone was hitting her. Nance heard her in the night. Got out of bed and went to be with her. But her mother pushed her away. My darling boy, she kept saying. Oh, my darling boy.

The letter came a few days later. Frank Russell had died of *dysentery and avitaminosis*. Dolly didn't know what that was. Starvation, Nance said. It means he died of starvation, Mum. She thought, How dare they dress it up.

He'd died in the PoW camp, in Thailand, on the eighth of April 1944. That was eighteen months ago. She tried to think back to what she'd been doing that day. Was it the day she'd read about the shortage of rubber and pictured him standing under a rubber tree thinking about his sister? You had to find some comfort, no matter how silly. Otherwise the grief ate you up and swallowed you.

Later the medals arrived in the post. Dolly came to her with the three little tinny things on her palm. Went to say something but the words dried up. By then some of the truth was starting to come out. Not only the terrible things the Japanese had done to the prisoners, though that was sickening. Worse was how it could have been different if the men in charge had been more competent and less arrogant. The British had taken so many Australian soldiers to fight in Europe that there weren't enough left to fight the Japanese. So much for the Mother Country. When the chips were down, Mother turned her back. But the Brits had made out it would be all right. Singapore could never fall. All that boasting. The general in charge had got away in a boat, gone home and got a medal.

If Frank had died saving someone, or striking a blow against the enemy, there'd be some sort of consolation. But the more the truth came out, the more you were left with nothing but bitterness. She knew now that what people called destiny was really the system everyone was part of. The ones on the top of the pile kept everyone thinking they could get ahead, when in fact ordinary people never had a chance. The generals and the politicians were all feathering their own nests. The newspapers and newsreels were mouthpieces for the people who ran things. They'd say whatever suited the big people, and everyone would believe them. Ken might have called himself a revolutionary, but she was the one who'd become the real radical.

After Frank's death she went through the days like a machine. Life happened at a great distance. She didn't want to eat, her clothes hung on her and her face in the mirror was gaunt. She went through the motions with the boys and pretended cheerfulness for their sakes, but knew her smiles were a grimace. The idea of starting a pharmacy was ridiculous. It was impossible to believe that anything mattered or that you could ever care about anything again.

Dolly had become a pathetic old woman wrecked by grief. She took to visiting a spiritualist down at Dee Why. She'd get the bus in the afternoon and come back pale and lined, her eyes still sunk back into her head with crying but something eased around her stiff mouth. Nance looked at the little messages that were supposed to be from Frank:

> *A soldier Boy to the war did go*
> *Fighting hard to beat the Foe*
> *A wonderful boy so loyal and true*
> *Always with his loved ones tender and true*
> *When you sit alone I am with you Mother*
> *Just to whisper in your ear*
> *Not goodbye just good night*
> *Love Frank*

Oh, she wished she could believe. *Not goodbye just good night.* The reality was that Frank was a few bones somewhere in the steamy dirt of Thailand, and everything that he'd been was gone, gone, gone.

Her father wrote to say he'd had a visit from a man called Wal Ward who'd worked on the Burma Railway, what they called The Line, alongside Frank. Wal had been Frank's mate. He was a man with a big heart. He thought it might help Bert to know how things had been with Frank. Russ tried to look after the younger men, Wal had told him. Made sure they kept the flies off their food. Vigilant about that sort of thing.

Wal told Bert about another mate of Frank's. This man, Ernie Chapman, had managed to keep his watch hidden from the Japanese. When Frank got sick, Ernie sold the watch to a guard. Ernie was living on a cupful of rice a day, like everyone else, Wal said. But all the money went to buy extra food for Frank.

Nance wanted to find Wal Ward so she could talk to a man who'd known Frank, who'd been his friend through so much suffering. Wanted to find Ernie Chapman, too. Would have gone down on her knees to thank him. But Bert hadn't thought to get any addresses. Wal Ward had walked away down the drive of Green Hills and disappeared into a world full of hundreds of other men called Ward or Chapman.

One Sunday she took the boys down to Mona Vale Beach, the shallow part among the rocks where the water was still. Lay back on the sand, closed her eyes so the world was the red of her eyelids, the thump and rattle of the waves sliding up the beach, the cries of the gulls. She might have slept for a moment. When she opened her eyes the world was colourless, white shapes and black shapes, unfamiliar, sinister. Where were the boys?

Nance lurched to her feet, stumbled in a panic down to the water's edge. They could be anywhere, sunk to the bottom with their lives ticking away. The noise of the surf covered everything. Stop, she thought, for God's sake, stop so I can hear them! She waded in, pushing against the solid dead mass that pushed back, heading to the shadowed part under the rocks where the water was dark and evil.

Then they were there, two shining brown bodies up on the rocks, running along with their hands full of something, tossing them into the air—shells, they must be—and screaming with laughter to see them rain down onto the still water. She stood watching them, stroking the surface of the water with her palms. It was silky, soft against her skin, a part of the lovely merciful world that had not taken her boys.

Later they came to where she was under the umbrella and lay on each side of her, their skins goose-bumped from the cold water. They fell asleep and for a long time she looked at the small things about them. The way the salt was drying on Christopher's arm in delicate lacework. The way Stephen's hair grew from two crowns, so that the hairs spiralled softly away from each centre like something stilled in the middle of moving.

Frank's hair had grown like that, from two crowns. Dolly had said it meant you were good at arithmetic. Like a gift, the thought came to her: Frank wasn't gone. He was right here, part of his nephews. The boys had some of Ken, and they had some of her. Through her they had some of Frank, too. The world had taken Frank, but it had given her these two. And a few minutes ago it had given them to her all over again.

She had to live the life that Frank had been robbed of. Live it in handfuls. Live all the possibilities, not turn away too timid or too sad or too weary, because that was the best way to honour Frank.

FIFTEEN

ULA BOUGHT the cottage and Nance drove to the city to order the stock. When she was near Central, in the middle of a complicated five-way intersection where three other cars were dithering about who should go first, the Essex stalled. She tried to look unconcerned, opening the door, getting down, folding back the bonnet. But as soon as she got out, horns started to blare and the men in other cars shouted at her. She closed her ears to the words, got the thing fiddled with, folded the bonnet back down, prayed the car would start. A man would have been forgiven, she thought, but not a woman.

At Faulding's the man behind the counter sent for the boss and the boss came down to have a look at this woman who thought she could start a pharmacy. Not buy one already going, not go into it with her husband—start it on her own! Nance had brought her new *Certificate of Registration* and it was good she had, because he asked to see it. He read every word, held it up to the light as if it must be a forgery.

Newport! He said. Too small. You won't be open a week.

In the end he had to give her the stock. But he wouldn't let her have it on credit. She knew pharmacists never paid cash, but he wouldn't budge. Sorry, madam, cash payment only, he kept saying. Oh, how she hated being called madam!

She got the little they could afford. Ula's daughter Deirdre turned out to have a knack for arranging things so they looked more than they were. It was Deirdre who had the idea of filling some of the empty pharmacy bottles. Sand, cut-up leaves, gumnuts squashed on the back step with a hammer. Put them along the shelves with a nice label in Latin and who was to know what was in them?

In the week before the shop opened, Ken nailed up signs everywhere: *Pharmacy Opening Monday*. He was a poor sort of a husband in many ways. But he didn't despise women the way so many men did. When she'd told him about the man in Faulding's, he'd called the fellow a maggot. He built the shelves in the shop, found a second-hand counter and hired a truck to get it up to Newport. It wasn't only that he wanted the money she was going to make. It was as he'd told her all those years ago: he admired her and esteemed her for having a profession, and for being a pioneer. He was proud of her and respected her for throwing aside convention.

She thought it might be what he'd married her for: her difference from the traditional idea of a woman. That included things he didn't know how to deal with—how she wanted more from him, emotionally, than he could give—but it also included her drive, her ambition, her ingenuity. In a way, she thought, it was the man in her that he liked.

On the day in October 1946 that Nance and Ula opened the doors, three customers were already waiting outside. A few minutes later a mother came in with her little boy and Ula did a lovely neat job of the big cut on his knee. Nance was on the go all day, out the back with the mortar, racing to get the stuff into the pill machine, the pills scooped into the bottle. She'd hear the shop door ping and ping again, and a swell of noise in the front room like a party, except it was customers waiting to be served.

At the end of the first week they could hardly believe the figures. Oh, you'd expect a rush at the start, the man at Faulding's said when Nance came back for more stock. Flash in the pan, mark my words.

Within a month the order was getting so big that it wasn't safe to carry so much cash. He had to give in and let her have credit. But no man would ever admit he was wrong, she thought. He always found something disparaging to say, and if all else failed he could come the big I-am in the yard getting the Essex started.

The shop opened at nine and shut at five during the week, and four hours on a Saturday morning. At first

they didn't open on Sunday but people came round to the
house and in the end it was easier to open for an hour,
so it was seven days a week. Still, compared to the hours
at Enmore it was heaven. Ula was a good nurse and was
often called out to a job. Then Nance was on her own
in the shop. How could she nut out the doctor's terrible
handwriting on the script, dispense a dose of chlorodyne,
weigh Mrs Phelan's baby and serve the woman wanting
calomine lotion, all at the same time, and keep smiling
the way a shopkeeper should?

Part of the problem was that a pharmacy could only
be open if the registered pharmacist was on the premises.
When Nance slipped over the road to the butcher to
get something for dinner she was breaking the law.
The inspector who'd signed the *Certificate of Compliance,
Pharmaceutical Premises* had made no secret of his belief
that a woman's place was at home. He'd spent two hours
in the shop, getting out his tape measure to make sure
the dispensing bench was the regulation size, measuring
the flow of water from the tap, checking that the *British
Pharmacopoeia* was on the premises as by law it had to be.
He even took it over to the window, peering to check
that it was the right edition. He'd love the chance to close
her down.

Dolly did as she'd promised, kept the house clean
and got the tea on the table. But there was so much else!
Nance felt some days that her brain would explode.
They'd run out of sultanas, vanilla, sugar. Christopher had
grown out of his shoes, the basket was full of mending,

Mr Goldsworthy's account was overdue, and she'd have to speak to the delivery boy about always being late. Oh, and mousetraps. And she hadn't reconciled the cheque-book for two weeks. She was a woman running ahead of a whirlwind.

She'd prepared herself for that. What took her by surprise was an uneasiness that was first cousin to guilt. When she was with the boys, half of her mind was still with the shop. But when she was in the shop she thought of the boys, their precious childhoods racing past. She loved her children but she loved to be out in the world too. How did you divide yourself?

When the magazine came home from Lakehouse School she was proud that the cover was a linocut by Stephen, a train with a hill and the sun rising, or perhaps setting. Christopher had a long story about flying in an aeroplane. He'd never been in an aeroplane but he'd imagined it vividly, a wonderful story for a boy only five years old. The ending was a jolt, though. *Soon when we got home Mummy went to work the day after. Daddy had to go to his office to make money and Mummy made a lot of money at her shop.* He didn't mean it as a reproach. But she had to fight the feeling that it was.

The shop had been going five months when Dolly told her she was leaving. Oh, Mum, why, Nance said, wanting to shout, But you promised! It's the everyday, Dolly said. You know, every day the same. It was what Nance had seen in her childhood: her mother's craving for change and challenge. There was no point arguing. It was her own fault, for fooling herself that this time would be different.

With her mother gone, the whirlwind caught up with Nance. It was half-past five by the time she got home with the boys. The house cold, the breakfast dishes not washed, and nothing to cook for tea unless she'd been able to snatch a moment during the day to slip out and get something. The boys tired and cranky, falling asleep in their dirty clothes, and no clean ones for the next day, and her white coat too dirty to go again but the other one still not dry.

When she said, Ken, I can't do it all on my own, he was astonished. But I help, he said. I help all the time!

I don't want help, she said. I want someone to think ahead the way I have to, and do it without me having to ask. Not just help! Afterwards she was sorry she'd spoken so harshly. She was in the right, but if she wasn't grateful for his help he mightn't do even the little he did. She thought, If it was me on my own I could go on strike, but the children are his hostages.

There was something wrong with the whole set-up, but she couldn't step back from it far enough to see what it was. She couldn't even seem to find the right words to talk about it. It was as if the situation was too strange or new for there to be a language to describe it. When she tried to explain, Ken said, What, do you want me to be the wife? And you the husband? She was silenced.

The winter school holiday was approaching. Lakehouse would be closed for three weeks. She asked everyone she knew if they could think of anyone who'd mind the boys. She put up notices in all the shop windows in Newport and Mona Vale. It was worth her whole profit to find someone and it would only be for three weeks, so she offered good money.

Ken told her that in Russia the government set up creches so women could go to work knowing their children would be properly cared for. Shame there's nothing like that here, isn't it, he said. That was the extent of his engagement with the problem.

Finally a woman responded. Nance didn't take to her, she was a huge slatternly woman, broken shoes and the kind of nose that suggested too much of the bottle. She'd look after the boys, but she'd only do it at her place. Nance had no choice. The school was closing the next day.

Each day when she picked the boys up from the woman's house their faces were pale and strained. The fourth day she stopped the car, took Stephen on her lap and put her arm around Christopher. It all came out. The woman was shutting them in a cupboard to keep them quiet.

She had to take them with her to the shop. They'd be in the back room, and it would be all right for the first hour or two. Stephen would make cubbies out of toilet-paper rolls and Christopher would work on his model plane. Then they'd start to squabble. She'd have to drop whatever she was doing to sort it out. When Ula was there she could help, but if she was out on a nursing job it was impossible.

School went back, but then there was a cold snap and both the boys got sick. She made a nest for them out in the back room, and went in to see to them when she could. But everyone else was sick too and the shop had never been so busy. Ula was away all day, banging people on the back to bring up the phlegm.

The boys lay like foundlings in their nest of cushions and blankets on the floor, watching their mother come in and out, in and out, with never the time to sit with them. At the end of the day, when she picked Stephen up, she saw that his cushions had separated. The poor thing had been lying on the boards. Why didn't you say? she asked, and heard her voice sounding sharper than she'd meant.

She knew why he hadn't said anything. He had protected her from his need because he'd seen how harassed she was. She stood in the back room holding him, a hot weight in her arms, and saw that her children must be coming to feel that the shop mattered more than they did. They were being bundled around with whoever would have them, parked away wherever they'd be quiet enough to let her work. It wasn't what a loving parent did.

If the business hadn't been so successful she'd have been able to manage. It was a sad irony. She'd thought she could make it work, but she'd been wrong.

The pharmacist Ula found to buy Nance out could hardly believe his luck. Nance tried to smile as she shook his hand. He was already behind the counter—her counter!—starting his first day in a lovely starched white coat. He had a wife at home, naturally, to do the washing and the starching. Not to mention the shopping and the dinners, and sweeping the floors and looking after the children.

It was hard to walk away from the thing that had got her living again after Frank's death. She couldn't face going home straight away and walked down to the beach, took off her shoes so she could feel the coarse yellow sand between her toes, sat on the dune among the pale stringy grass. The waves rolled in, each one different and each one the same. It was good not to think about anything, not to do anything but watch. Big waves and small ones, crooked ones and long straight ones. Waves swelling and folding under themselves, a neat quick line of foam running and disappearing, and always another one behind it, swelling and glittering and folding under itself.

By the time she got up and brushed the sand off the back of her skirt she could see it all in a better light. She'd made seven hundred pounds. After less than a year, that was what the goodwill had been worth! It would give them most of what they needed for a modest house. Something else: she'd proved it could be done. A woman could open a pharmacy and make decent money. She'd proved that she was that woman. She'd done it once, she could do it again. She just had to be patient. When you're a woman, she thought, you *can* do everything. Just not all at the same time.

SIXTEEN

THEY GOT a couple of builders to quote. Six hundred pounds was the lowest, and that was only for the labour, no materials. They see a professional man, think they can get away with anything, Ken said. I know the tricks these grimy-handed toilers get up to. Oh, how he loved giving a sardonic twist now to the old Trotskyite phrases.

He had an idea even more outlandish than a woman starting a pharmacy: they'd build the house themselves. Why not, he said. Remember, Nance, I'm not only a lawyer, I'm a Dilutee Fitter and Turner too! He was laughing at himself, but she knew him well enough now to see he was going to do it. She thought the two of them weren't so very different. If things were in line by a few more degrees they might have had a happy marriage.

He sent away for a dense little book, *How to Build Your Own Home*, and one Saturday in March 1948 he brought the mattock down into the soft dark soil.

He made a little ceremony of it: the Turning of the First Sod. She turned the second. They helped Christopher do the third and Stephen the fourth. Other families go to church together, she thought, or play charades together. The Gee family turns the first sod together.

By the time Ken went back to Sullivans on the Monday the trenches were dug, but that was the only easy part. Building materials were still in short supply after the war and there were no bricks to be had for the foundations. That was Chapter Two, 'Footings and Piers'. The trench filled up with rainwater and weeds sprouted along the edges. She had to remind herself that it was no more absurd to imagine a house rising up from those puddles than it had been to imagine a pharmacy at Newport.

One Saturday, Ken came in with a bucket full of rough clay. Look, Nance, he said. Got this down by Louis' creek. The Medes and Persians did it. Or was it the Israelites?

There was nothing in *How to Build Your Own Home* about making your own bricks but you could put together a surprising amount of information from Exodus. All that time at the convent hadn't been a waste after all. She went off to Homer's dairy and arranged for him to deliver a bale of straw. She pretended it was for strawberries.

Ken made two wooden moulds for what he proudly called the *prototypes* and they mixed up the clay and the straw. The boys loved it: mud pies with a purpose. The next

Saturday, when the bricks were as dry as the sun could make them, Ken put them in the kitchen oven. A couple of hours later he took one out. It looked like a real brick but it crumbled in his hand.

It was some bit of a fiddle, Ken never told her the full story, but one day there were the bricks in a tidy stack by the side of the road. He told her he'd been spending his lunch hours during the week watching bricklayers at work. He'd get them in conversation, he boasted, and they'd be so flattered at the interest that they'd show him all the tricks of the trade. Nance saw that it was the lure of the secret world again, one thing on the surface and another hidden away below.

There was a little smile at the corners of his mouth as he buttered up the end of each brick, tapped it into place with the handle of the trowel and scraped the excess off with a flourish. No doubt about it, she thought. He'd been born into the wrong sort of family. As a bricklayer or a carpenter he'd have been a happier man.

He did as much as he could that weekend, then he showed Nance how to do it. She was surprised at how easy it was. The mortar was a lovely creamy consistency and laying it on was like icing a cake. On the Monday, when he had to get into his suit and catch the bus into town, she took the boys to school, then came back and put on her overalls and old boots and got to work.

All week, people passing stopped to marvel. She'd wave up at them and then go back to work as if there was nothing out of the ordinary. Why shouldn't a woman lay bricks? The world would never change if someone wasn't prepared to be the first.

Ria came one day with scones and a thermos. Nance, you're a remarkable woman, she said. A really remarkable woman. Nance thought, Well, perhaps I am. She was pleased that the boys were seeing her doing it. They'll be better husbands, she thought. They'll know what women are capable of.

Chapter Three was 'Timber Framing', but they couldn't get timber. People warned her there'd be none, oh, not for years. People were such nay-sayers! *Cast your bread upon the waters*, she'd say, and pretend not to care.

The bread upon the waters returned in the form of Mr Ferguson who lived further along the road. He was Ferguson Steel, he was making a fortune, had the best house in the street and three cars. She was standing among the piers one day when he picked his way down the block to her.

Been watching you do those, he said. Done a bloody good job, Mrs Gee. Listen, I'll give you a discount on a steel frame. And give you the roof for nothing.

She smiled up at his silhouette, the sun in her eyes. Was he pulling her leg?

One condition, he said. You let me take a photo of you and your husband building with the steel. He spread his hands out as if holding up a newspaper. 'So simple even a lawyer and his wife can do it!'

When the *Sun* came, a reporter and a photographer, they made her get up on the roof and pretend to bang away at the nails. 'Wife Helps to Build Home', the caption read. What did they mean, *help*? But in the story Ken said, 'My wife laid all the brick piers and is helping with the flooring. Through the week she spends her spare time driving nails into the floorboards.' It made nailing floorboards sound like embroidery, but he'd given her full credit. Many a man wouldn't have.

Seeing themselves written up, oddities worth a quarter of a page, made her realise she hadn't done so badly in choosing Ken. He was disappointing in so many ways. But Wal Glendon wouldn't have sent away for a book about how to build a house. Nor would Charlie Gledhill. Even if they had, they wouldn't have been proud of having a wife who could nail floorboards.

The person they didn't mention in the *Sun* was Louis. Once the frame was delivered, Ken employed Louis as a day labourer. Together Louis and Nance came to hate Ferguson's steel. The frame was like giant Meccano and unforgiving. Ferguson called it *nailable steel*, and it was, but only with a terrible lot of fiddling around. You had to find the exact slit in the steel. It nipped your fingers and left your hands black with grease.

Louis spoke to the rotten steel in German. He never shouted but the long lumpy strings of sounds were all the more menacing for that. She remembered that poor teacher at Tamworth High who'd lasted a fortnight. *With every language learned, man gains a soul.* Louis speaking German was another man, and it was the words of that other language that shaped him. People said German was an ugly language, but listening to Louis talking to the steel she found it mysterious and attractive.

What are you saying, Louis, she said. Louis had a lovely smile, warm and frank.

Nance, he said, I could not dirty your ears with what I told this damn stuff.

What, she said, worse than *Himmel donnerwetter*? I know you told me damn and blast, but what does it mean, the actual words?

Himmel, that's heaven, he said. *Donnerwetter*, that's a thunderstorm. He laughed. Heaven thunderstorm! Silly, isn't it.

The two of them grew close, working side by side all day. She came to love the way he looked at her when he'd said something funny and was waiting for her to laugh. The joke was a kind of caress at a distance.

She knew he fancied her, even in the terrible old overalls and the flannel shirt, her hair wrapped in a scarf and her face shiny from the struggle with the steel. He gave her the feeling she hadn't had for a long time, that she was desirable. A desirable and interesting woman who could make a man laugh and look at her in a tender admiring way. For Louis, the entirety of her was desirable, her body and her mind and the whole muddle of things that made her the person she was.

They were from the opposite sides of the globe but they were from the same world. Louis' father was a railway fettler, his mother a peasant who could make anything from a potato. Louis had only had a few years' schooling, ran away to the merchant navy to escape from a hungry Germany, jumped ship when he got to Sydney. In Australia he'd been a dairy farmer, a butler, an extra in the movies, a tablecloth salesman. He was in awe of Nance's education, the way she'd been in awe of Ken's.

For lunch they'd go down to Louis' place among the banana trees and boil the kettle on his Primus. She liked his small neat house, one room really, the scrubbed table in the middle with the two chairs and the narrow bed in the corner with the crocheted coverlet. They'd put the wireless on and listen to the news, but one day they were too late for the news and it was dance music. May I have this dance, madame? She loved the way Louis called her *madame*. Not madam, like those awful men at Faulding's, but *madame* in the French way.

It was the most natural thing in the world to find themselves one day on the bed. Even there, ripening tomatoes lined up on the windowsill beside them, he was making her laugh. Absurd, he mumbled into her shoulder. This nun's bed! These damn tomatoes watching us! She hadn't laughed, doing it, since Charlie Gledhill on the blanket out in the bush.

There was nothing in it. They didn't even need to have the conversation. They both knew that there was no happiness in her marriage, and that she wasn't going to leave it, because of the boys. But if she had to live the rest of her life without that loving connection to another human being, she thought, something in her would die, as it had in her mother. If you denied the animal pleasures, the animal bonds, the connection of one soul to another, you were half dead, trudging pointlessly through life. It was life's power and pleasure moving through her when she lay with Louis, and it would keep her alive.

No one would ever know and be hurt by what was happening on the nun's bed. She would make sure of that. It was as they said about lighting one candle from another: one gains everything and the other loses nothing. She and Louis knew the same truth: life was short. It had its hard times and its sad times. All a person could do was to enjoy whatever there was to be enjoyed. Which, for a time in quiet Crescent Road, with the banana leaves scraping together and the magpies carolling, was each other.

Once the building was finished, so was the closeness. Louis still came up to the new house on a Saturday afternoon to spruce up. Still danced with her in the kitchen. There was an extra, affectionate depth now to the warmth between them. Something lovely had happened. Now it was over. It was exactly as he'd promised: bubbles and love, and no headache in the morning.

SEVENTEEN

THEY CALLED the house Bringalilli, in memory of Frank. The place in Queensland had been his first real home since he'd left Rothsay as a boy of seven. This place was the same for her. So many years of pubs, boarding houses, rented places. Other people's furniture and saucepans, and always the worry at the back of your mind: have we got this week's rent?

With no mortgage and no rent, and Ken's steady money from Sullivans, for the first time in her adult life Nance didn't have to worry about money. All around her she saw people who'd been through the Depression the way she had, who'd become frightened of spending money. Something in them had become shrunken and fearful. Even when they had plenty, money still ruled their lives. They kept their nice things for best, stinted themselves in small meaningless ways. She'd taken a different lesson from those hard years. When you didn't have money, you made the best of things. Once you'd gone without, you knew you could manage. But when you had it, you should enjoy it.

She wasn't interested in becoming a late-in-the-day lady or in spending money to impress other people. She wanted the kind of small functional luxuries that made ordinary days a pleasure. Good knives and forks, the feel of quality sheets on the bed, furniture that was comfortable but robust enough that you didn't have to fiddle around with coasters and antimacassars.

A piano was still beyond their means, but she found a second-hand pedal organ that she thought would get the boys started, and took them every week to lessons. Took them to the local C of E church most Sundays. Not because she believed in anything beyond the world she knew, but because every child should know the Bible. It was like knowing those lines from Shakespeare and Keats. Without that sense of what other people had created, without a connection to that body of tradition, you were a floating nothing.

Guyda was right, the boys were reading and writing and doing sums. Still, Nance thought it was time they went to a proper school. Otherwise the rules and regulations of high school would be too much of a shock. The house was halfway between the public school at Newport and the one at Mona Vale, but she heard something about the teacher at Newport that struck her as barbaric, though she'd seen it done in her own childhood: left-handers had that hand tied behind their backs to force them not to write with it.

The boys started at Mona Vale Public. Each morning she watched them pedal off on their bikes down Crescent Road, out into the world. She saw, with sadness, that family gave meaning to life, but it couldn't be forever. Your children are just on loan to you, she thought. You have to be worthy of the loan and do your very best for them. Then you have to be willing to let them fly away into their own lives. It wasn't happening yet, but she could see that it would come. That will be my last gift to them, she thought: to let them go.

She'd turn back into the house, with nothing much to do until it was time to wait for them at the gate in the afternoon with milk and biscuits ready on the table. She laughed at herself with the other mothers. Oh, I don't know myself now, she'd say. I'm a lady of leisure! They looked at her strangely when she said it. It took her a while to realise that doing nothing but keeping house and looking after children felt like a holiday to her, but for them it was a full-time job. *Lady of leisure.* They probably thought she was laughing at them.

She had time now to read. For a while she bought the women's magazines, but she soon became impatient with them. Kings and queens! She couldn't care less. She ended up subscribing to the *Saturday Evening Post.* She liked the stories and poems and the articles about ideas that were new to her. More than once she thought, I could write a piece about something, but perhaps it was that good writers made it look easy.

Words had been her first love, Keats in that hot classroom with Mr Crisp, entering the mind of a poet more than a hundred years dead. Mr Crisp had helped her glimpse that literature was more than entertainment. It was a kind of instruction manual for life, circling the great glowing mystery at the centre, the mystery of being human. You were alive for such a short time and then you went back into the great silence. The only ones who didn't vanish were the artists. While you were reading their words and looking at their pictures they were still alive, and you shared some of their life too.

Other people had religion to give them a connection to eternity, and good luck to them, but religion was too narrow for her, too unforgiving, too literal. Literature encompassed everything, forbade nothing, endorsed nothing. Writers, like scientists, had the greatest respect for the world as it truly was. Their job wasn't to judge but to examine, to experiment, draft after draft, century after century.

She read the writers praised by the reviewers: Huxley, Waugh, Snow, Greene, Hemingway. She was amused by sly Waugh, recognised something from her own experiences in earnest Snow. But the world of these writers was the world of men: politics and war and *cherchez la femme*. Women had no place except as objects men desired or didn't desire. To enter the world of their books, she had to temporarily turn herself into a man.

Ria lent her a translation of *Madame Bovary*. Perhaps the French had a different view of things: she thought

Flaubert didn't like women much, but for all her silliness Emma Bovary was a full human being with a complicated internal life, not just a set of surfaces that a man might or might not find desirable.

She expected women writers to understand more than men, and some of them did. They knew that, in a world run by men, marriage could only be a strategy to survive. It was nasty but it was simple. For Jane Austen's women, husbands were meal tickets. These days it's more confusing, she thought. A woman like me who's her own meal ticket doesn't know how to choose. That's what got so many of us into a bad situation. For men, though, nothing has changed. They still marry for the reasons they always did: sex on tap and a free housekeeper.

But even the women writers didn't go very far in understanding the real heart of a woman's life, because most of them had never been married. They were like men in not knowing the most basic things: how it felt to be financially dependent, to create and nurture children, to be obliged to find satisfaction in the narrow world of the home. Yet what could be more dramatic than surrendering your autonomy? What could be more profound than the bond between a parent and a child? The intensity and complexity of that relationship made mere romantic love look shallow.

One Saturday the paper carried a review of a book by a writer called Elizabeth Taylor. *Her dinners burn and her children mess themselves embarrassingly. She has an exact eye for trivial domestic detail.* No book Nance had ever read described burned dinners or messed children. None had even mentioned trivial domestic details, let alone been exact about them.

The night Ken brought the novel home for her she burned their own dinner, reading in the kitchen, so engrossed that she didn't smell the potatoes until they were almost alight. *At Mrs Lippincote's* was about the world she knew: the invisible armies of disregarded mothers and housewives. Elizabeth Taylor proved what Nance had always known, that the quiet domestic dramas of women's lives might be invisible to men, but they mattered just as much.

Apart from his eighteen months as a proletarian, Ken had been a solicitor for ten years. The work at Sullivans was more interesting than probate and conveyancing but it didn't fully engage him. The only times he came to life were when Sullivans represented a client themselves rather than briefing a barrister. Appearing in court called for the kind of quick ingenuity he loved. *The cut and thrust,* he called it. He'd come home exhilarated and boast to Nance about the traps he'd set in cross-questioning. The best way to rattle a male witness was apparently to start by asking them the dates of their children's birthdays. Usually they didn't know and it threw them off balance. The best way to make witnesses blurt things out was to leave a silence. It was the excitement she'd seen in him before. Being on the inside, having the secret knowledge.

So when he came to her one day and said, Nance, I'm thinking of going to the Bar, she thought, Yes, he's got to do this. She'd come to understand that there was something romantic, even flamboyant, in his nature. It was what had got him into the Trotskyites: big ideas, big ambitions, big secrets. He was thirty-four. Too old to have too many more fresh starts left in him, but too young to look down the years and see no chance to live a larger life.

You know, Nance, he said, there might be less money for a while.

She'd already thought of that. I'll go back to Quinn's for a year, she said. Give you a chance to get established. It's no good being miserable.

He thanked her, sincerely. He did have some idea what working at Quinn's was like. Mr Quinn had been smug when she'd had to sell her Newport business. Well, Mrs Gee, he'd said, unable to keep the triumph out of his voice, you know you're welcome back here at any time.

Going back to work for him would be to eat the humblest of pies. Surely, though, it wouldn't be for long. All Ken's colleagues from Sullivans and the old comrades from the Trotsky days would send plenty of work his way.

With the boys older and the war finished, it was easier to make domestic arrangements. Miss Bowden down the road had worked during the war but once the men came back she'd been let go. Nance gave her three pounds a week, a quarter of what she got at Quinn's.

Miss Bowden minded the boys when they got home from school and got dinner ready. Nance missed those hours after school with the boys, but it would only be for the year, less if Ken got plenty of work straight away.

Another big slice of her pay went into the new machines to keep food cold or suck the dirt off the floors. She'd always liked the iceman with his great tongs holding the block, the tunnels of air like beads through the ice. She apologised to him. All the people like her who were buying fridges were doing him out of a job. But how much easier not to have to worry about the ice melting, and mopping up where the icebox was always leaking!

A woman a few doors along got a washing machine and all the women in the street crowded into her laundry to watch the miracle. You dropped the clothes in and turned the machine on. When you came back, the washing was done! But Nance didn't think the little paddle feebly agitating the water would get the clothes properly clean. She knew from the ads in the *Saturday Evening Post* that there were machines in America where you put the clothes in the front, so that gravity moved them around. She was going to wait till they were available in Australia.

Ken was shocked at how much the machines cost. But he'd never washed a shirt or had to worry about keeping the milk fresh. Your mother had a maid and a cook, she said. Well, these things are the new servants. He wasn't convinced, but he didn't have to be. It was her money. Still, even with everything so much easier than it had been last time she'd worked, Nance once again had her day divided into small segments of time, each with its task.

Ken went to his chambers every day and waited for briefs, but they never came. After all his grand plans he grew silent, his face dark with humiliation. Why weren't those comrades sending him work, Nance wondered. He was clever, ingenious in argument, spoke well and wittily. He worked as hard as anyone she knew. It was something else. She'd watched him doing that gusty banter that men did, that empty camaraderie. It was as if he'd learned it out of a book. The others picked it up: the scent of the outsider. They were affable with him, but not truly friends.

She couldn't ask about his empty days. She couldn't talk about how much she hated working at Quinn's, either, because that would seem like a reproach. She put a brave face on it, but it was awful. Everyone pitied her for having a husband who couldn't support her.

He came home one day with a bounce in his step and she thought he must finally have landed a case, but it was a different kind of triumph: he'd had a story published in the *Mirror*. There it was on page ten: 'Chinaman's Cave', by Kenneth Gray. Oh, nothing much, he said. A rattling good yarn, that's all.

The story was about a man who steals jewels from a Chinese hermit but then fears that he's caught leprosy from him.

For peace of mind, for relief from the fear that never leaves me, I would gladly give up every penny I possess. I am worth perhaps fifty thousand pounds, in addition to the many coins and golden ornaments that I have not yet sold. That was my share of the find; Wilson took the rest.

I've got you to thank for the idea, Ken said. You know, the Coast Hospital.

Oh, those poor old lepers! She hoped they didn't read the *Mirror*.

He had to write under a nom de plume, he told her, because barristers weren't allowed to advertise, and publishing a story was a kind of advertising. But she thought it was really the lure of secrecy, of going through the world unrecognised, a man no one looked at twice, but who carried in his brain the seeds of grand things.

He was paid two pounds twelve and six for 'Chinaman's Cave'. She wondered if he thought it was a career, the journalist dream from his young days made real. Two more stories were published in quick succession and he wrote others. She glimpsed the scribbled-over typescripts. But there were no more triumphant copies of the *Mirror* and no more cheques for two pounds twelve and six.

She was surprised at how gentle she felt, how careful not to ask. It's the same way I am with the boys, she thought. Saving his pride. Ken seemed strong, but in protecting him she recognised what she'd always known: she was stronger than he was.

Halfway through 1949 the coalminers went on strike. Nance sympathised. Imagine spending your life underground! The least you could ask for was decent pay. Ken brushed that aside. The strike was just a tactic, he said, by the communists who ran the union. They wanted to bring down the government. Why, she asked, when it's a Labor government? Ken explained that the communists hated Labor, because Labor held out the possibility of reform without revolution. He knew their tricks, he said. When he was a Trotskyite he'd done the same. It was a cold surprise to Nance to hear him laugh at the poor miners for being nothing more than the dupes of the reds.

When Chifley sent the army in to break the strike, Ken cheered. Labor had finally found its spine. But Nance was horrified. A Labor government sending in soldiers against working men! It was the first time she was willing to take Ken on about politics. Some things you could be sure about, just because you were human.

You are a cold fish, Ken, she shouted. A cold bloody fish with no proper feelings! The accusation surprised him, but she could see that it confirmed his view that, under her competence and intelligence, his wife was just another emoting woman.

Now that Labor had come to its senses Ken rejoined and started going to meetings again. One night he came home and told her the party had asked him to stand at the next election. He was now the Labor candidate for the newly created seat of Bradfield.

She found it hard to believe. Bradfield? It would be the safest Liberal seat in the country, part of the upper North Shore, where all those years ago her father had sold sugar and biscuits to the born-to-rule lot. Not only that, but Ken would be up against the grand old man of conservative politics, Billy Hughes. Ken Gee standing against the Little Digger: it was the quixotic gesture again, the perverse glamour of the lost cause.

He doorknocked, spoke at public meetings, wrote letters to the paper, stayed in town late into the evenings at the Trades Hall. Nance went on working at Quinn's. That gave her a good excuse not to help him with the doorknocking. Two weeks before the election, though, he talked her into coming with him to a public meeting. You're a great asset to me, Nance, he said. You know, the human face of the candidate.

When they arrived at the meeting someone gave her a huge bouquet and everyone clapped. She met Ken's eye around the flowers. He was smiling, proud of her. *The human face of the candidate.* The flowers were a nuisance, she didn't know whether you were supposed to go on holding them. She hadn't realised she'd be sitting up on the stage with the speakers and started to worry that she'd be asked to do something, pick the raffle or cut a cake. Wished she'd worn her good shoes. She'd come straight from work and her shabby old shoes were right on the level of the audience. Well, she thought, perhaps it's best, I never trusted Guido because of his expensive Italian footwear.

She tucked her feet under the chair and tried to listen to the speeches, but she was tired. Whatever you do, don't fall asleep, she told herself. And she should have put the flowers down somewhere straight away. That's what Queen Mary did when someone gave her flowers, passed them straight back to one of the flunkies. When Ken got up to speak he was forceful and lively, made some witty remarks that got everyone laughing. If she didn't know that he could just as easily turn all his lawyer's tricks to arguing for the other side, she might have believed he was a man of real conviction.

By eight in the morning on election day she was standing at the gate of St Ives Public School with a stack of how-to-vote cards. She'd brought a basket with a big thermos of tea and sandwiches. Ken said, It's not a picnic, Nance! But she knew she'd be stuck there all day while he was running around *putting in an appearance* at the polling places. Beside her was a man handing out Liberal Party cards for Billy Hughes and further along a woman was handing them out for an independent called Edward Price. She made sure she said good morning, to show there was nothing personal. The Price woman looked haughty, as if it was a trap, but the Liberal man smiled and let her have first go at people as they came along.

It was peculiar, handing out your husband's face to strangers. He looked intense, reserved, glancing sideways. He'd made sure that the photo only showed his face, not his bald crown. If she didn't know him, would she vote for him? Some voters brushed past her as if they were offended to be offered the card. Others looked solemn, taking their democratic duty seriously, accepting a card for each of the candidates. When the first flurry thinned out the Liberal man met her eye. Funny, aren't they, he said. They want to keep us guessing!

By eleven o'clock she was gasping for a cup of tea, got the thermos out of the basket. From the corner of her eye she saw the Liberal man glance at her and then glance away. You'll have to use the same cup, she said. But you look as if you could do with a hot drink.

He said no, but she could tell he was dying for it. Finally he took the cup and when she unwrapped the egg and lettuce sandwiches he let himself be persuaded to have one of those too. I came without anything, he kept saying. I never thought. She'd brought plenty. She'd often found she was the only one who'd thought of the practicalities. He was a cheerful pleasant man and obviously thought the same of her because after he'd thanked her he said, How can a nice woman like you be mixed up with the Labor Party?

I'm a working woman, she said. I believe in what the Labor Party stands for. She knew about missing out, about people having no choices and no chances and no proper education to give them any. She knew how people were cheated and hoodwinked by the ones with the power. Perhaps it was naïve to think like that. The Hughes man wasn't impressed. But it was what she believed, what she'd learned from life.

Still, she couldn't pretend it was why she was here. She glanced at Ken's face in her hand. Well, she said, and he's my husband.

Eight thousand, six hundred and forty-five people chose to vote for Ken Gee against the man he called the Little Bugger. She heard him on the phone: I got a quarter of the votes! He didn't seem dispirited not to have won. But there was no talk of Labor setting him up next time with a seat he had a chance of winning. Nance thought it was the Trotsky business. They'd never really trust him.

He didn't talk about what he was going to do next. But he came back from town one day and she saw straight away that something had changed again. He'd heard around the traps that the Chief Crown Prosecutor was being sent to Manus Island to do the war-crimes trials. That left a gap among the Crown Prosecutors. The long and short of it was, Ken had the job: Acting Crown Prosecutor.

In her heart she thanked Frank. Those men being tried at Manus were the ones who'd killed him. If they hadn't been so cruel, he wouldn't be dead. But if they hadn't been so cruel, there'd be no job for Ken.

She went on working, but a few months later one of the other prosecutors dropped dead and Ken was taken on as a permanent Crown Prosecutor. To go to Quinn and tell him she was resigning was the best half-hour she'd had for a long time. Not that he was impressed.

Remember, Mrs Gee, there's always a spot for you here, he said, and she had to smile and thank him. After all, what Quinn so obviously thought might be right: Ken would get some other idea into his head and they'd need the twelve pounds ten again.

Being a Crown Prosecutor was a comedown for a man who'd thought he could be Australia's Lenin, who'd given Billy Hughes a run for his money, who'd seen himself striding the stage of the Sydney Bar. This was a job, you were a public servant, you got a salary like any pen-pushing bureaucrat. She feared Ken would become mean and silent, forced to inhabit a small life.

No, he was elated. You'd have thought his highest ambition had always been to be a Crown Prosecutor. She thought of the pain of her own thwarted schemes, the shop in Newport that she still couldn't pass without a pang. She was strong enough to let herself feel the pang and suffer it, but Ken's way was to change his colour like a chameleon, forget that he'd ever wanted something and not been able to have it. She envied his ability never to look back, never regret.

Ken threw himself into the job. It took him away from home five days a week on the country circuit. Grafton, Goulburn, Bathurst, Broken Hill. He was stimulated by the world of the bizarre that the job plunged him into. Husbands running amok with shotguns. Wives putting rat poison in the pumpkin scones. Men who did unthinkable things with sheep. As prosecutor it was his job always to find the worst, to probe and tease and trick until every last degrading detail was out in the light. All men are animals, he said, and he didn't mean they were loyal or affectionate like a dog. He meant they were driven by dark dreadful cravings.

There was a relish in the way he told her the worst things, pride in the way he felt he was seeing the authentic ugly underbelly of the world, while everyone else lived with cosy illusions. Once again he was the man who knew things that everyone else didn't.

Nance was on her own all week. She and the boys had their routines and their jokes and when Ken was home at the weekend he was like a visitor. The jokes had to be explained. But being away so much suited Ken. The part of him that was comfortable on his own was given free rein. Nance had to admit that it suited her too. She often thought about Dolly running Beach House at Newport while Bert was at the shop all week. There was something depressing about repeating your parents' pattern: a marriage in which you were just as happy apart as together. Still, it was a kind of freedom too.

In the end it wasn't lipstick on Ken's collar but the scent of some other woman's perfume through his clothes when he came back from Grafton. Yes, the pyjamas too. She stood in the laundry with them in her hand, the garden a rectangle of brightness through the doorway. A woman in Grafton. There was no surprise, only a bleak sort of satisfaction. Something clicking into place.

I ought to be upset, she thought. But how can I be, when really I've known all along?

Yet she noticed she was crankier with the children that afternoon. Burned the potatoes and swore at them smoking in the pan. The boys were so surprised they stopped and stared. She didn't say anything to Ken when he got home. She wasn't sure what to do. In the meantime, the secret knowing was a small revenge.

She didn't think she'd given him any sign that she knew. But why else did he turn to her in bed that night and say, Nance, there's something I've got to tell you. It's all over now, but I was seeing a woman.

He told her everything. Not that she asked or even wanted to know. It was that he wanted to tell her. The woman had thrown herself at him, he said. Desperate for a man, poor thing, and Nance, I'm a week reed. He actually laughed. She was nothing but a passing whim, he said. He promised that it was all over, that it would never happen again, that it had meant nothing. Begged her to forgive him. She waited for him to say it, and he did: All men are animals, after all.

She listened to the fluent confessions, the fluent regrets, the fluent promises. Even in the remorse and the apologies she could hear something that was almost a boast.

Why are you telling me, Ken, she wondered. If you've found someone else the way I did, to keep yourself alive, you don't need to tell. If you have to tell, it must be a kind of performance.

She thought, I'll know it's serious when he doesn't confess.

She didn't cry. There was a stoniness where the tears should have been. She'd lived for a long time with the pain of having a husband who didn't love her. That sting was old and dull. There was a certain dignity in going along as if you had no suspicion. But once you were told, you became a character in the other person's drama. You could be the wife who forgave, or the wife who didn't forgive, but either way you were part of a drama that belonged to him.

And what if she didn't forgive? She'd have to get out of bed, the heartbroken wife full of righteous anger. Spend the night on the couch, and next day dismantle the life they had together. *A broken home.* How could you tell the children? How could it not be terrible for them?

She felt no need to tell him about Louis or Charlie. She didn't want to play the game of tit for tat. Still, the woman in Grafton and all that she represented made her glad she'd known that painful love for Charlie. It was life, that pain. And she was glad she'd seized the day with Louis. That pleasure was life, too.

For a while Ken was different. Talking with her, making her laugh, showing interest in all her little doings. She didn't believe he'd really changed. You'll have to woo me properly, she thought. After a week he dropped the effort and withdrew again. She was glad she hadn't been too quick to believe him.

She asked herself whether she still loved Ken And she had to admit that, in spite of everything, the answer was yes. No one had ever engaged her heart and mind the way he did when he laid himself out to please. No one could pain her the way he did when he turned away.

During the long afternoons in the empty house she'd put a record on the gramophone. There were others she liked, but 'Smoke Gets in Your Eyes' was still her favourite. Alone except for the dog staring in amazement, she'd sing, pretending that deep lush voice, with the little catch on the final words, was her own.

It had been a lovely flame, what she'd felt for Ken. Now it was only smoke and the tears in her eyes. She'd let the flame fade into an ember because there was too much pain in trying to interest a man who didn't want to be interested. If he truly turned his attention on her again, she knew the flame would burn as bright as the night they'd met. But she knew that wasn't going to happen. Whatever she could offer a man, it wasn't what Ken wanted.

But they'd made something solid together. They had a marriage and all the tendrils of social connection that went with being husband and wife. They had the children they'd made together, and it wasn't too late to have another. On both sides there was admiration and esteem. There was the affection that springs from knowing another person day and night for ten years. These were not nothing.

She thought Ken must see it in the same way. And if you had a *passing thing* with a woman in Grafton it could be useful to have a wife in the background. She and Ken would go on, she thought. He'd have other women and confess, and she'd accept the confessions. It would be what they called a *modus vivendi*. Far from perfect, but workable. And with space for each of them to find meaning somewhere else.

She'd like another child. It wasn't too late, and Ken wouldn't care much one way or the other. He loved his children, but they were just the background to his days, whereas for her they filled the foreground, the middle and the background. Without them, the frame of her life would be empty.

When she knew she was pregnant for the third time she felt a great flush of joy. One last child, she thought. In spite of everything, what a lucky woman I am.

POSTSCRIPT

ONE OF my earliest memories is of watching my mother in a white coat weighing babies on the scales near the door of her second pharmacy. The shop was always busy. I'd sit on the floor behind the counter and get through most of a packet of barley sugar before she had time to notice. She'd be weighing the babies, typing up the labels for medicine bottles, going out the back to grind something in the mortar, inspecting someone's rash, putting the thermometer in someone's mouth.

I was born at Mona Vale in 1950, the year Ken became a Crown Prosecutor. Nance was thirty-eight. Two years later, when Christopher was eleven and Stephen was nine, the family moved to North Sydney, closer to the city, where the good high schools were. A year or two later Nance saw the opportunity to start a pharmacy in the new shopping centre at North Balgowlah.

It lasted longer than the one at Newport had, about

two years. Again it was the lack of child care that beat her. She had a partner, a young man who was supposed to take over from her at two o'clock so she could pick me up from school. At first he got there on time but after a while he became unreliable. I remember the days she was late. The teacher would have to wait with me at the school gate. Everyone else would have gone home and the playground would have a frightening empty look. The teacher would be cranky. Over my head I'd hear her sigh and complain to another teacher, Mrs Gee's late again. I'd be swallowing back the tears. One terrible afternoon it grew so late that I had to be taken into the staff room, full of cigarette smoke and unwelcoming faces.

There was no after-school care in 1955 because mothers weren't thought of as people who went out to work. Actually, quite a few did. But, no matter how many of them there were, they were somehow exceptions. Nothing was made easy for them and they had to make whatever improvised arrangements they could. For Nance the difficulties were compounded by the fact that the business was hers and its success or failure was up to her.

In the end she sold the pharmacy. She never let me see how much she regretted having to do it. It's only now that I can imagine what a narrowing of her life it was, to turn from being a successful businesswoman back to home duties.

Still, she threw herself into being an at-home mother. She helped us with our homework, made us practise the piano, sewed most of our clothes, organised birthday parties for us. She played hostess for Ken's colleagues at cocktail parties and dinners, learning new ways of cooking from *Oh, for a French Wife!* which among other things explained that it was the CO_2 and the volatile oils in a martini that made it work. That appealed to the pharmacist in her.

As a mother she was energetic, loving, bossy, sometimes embarrassing. She made us wear hats and zinc cream decades before melanoma was a word everyone knew. Made us eat Vogel's bread when it was still an eccentric little brick that came in a cellophane wrapper with a picture of ancient but healthy Dr Vogel. Our dentist was a heavily accented Viennese man whose family had been in the death camps. Dr Raubitschek didn't have an assistant, so my mother would stand beside the chair mixing up the old-fashioned mercury amalgam on a little glass block. She'd take off her wedding ring first, and I remember the pleasure she took in explaining the chemistry that caused mercury to destroy gold.

When I was nine she went on a tour, organised by a group of pharmacists, to what was then called Ayer's Rock. Central Australia wasn't a place many tourists went to in 1959. It was hard to get to, the conditions were primitive, and most Australians couldn't see why you'd bother. They'd rather go to London.

It was a trip that changed her thinking about the place she called home.

She'd been proud of being fifth-generation Australian, but in the Centre she saw people who were five-hundredth- or five-thousandth-generation Australian. In the country towns where she'd grown up there'd been people of Aboriginal descent all around her, but this was the first time she'd been aware of Indigenous people living on their traditional country, speaking their own languages.

Bill Harney, the ranger at the Rock, told the group his version of some Aboriginal stories about the place. That cleft in the Rock was the place where the Great Earth Mother had struck it with her digging stick, he said. Nance looked where he was pointing and saw the water seeping down the rock. That was the very water that the Great Earth Mother had brought forth. It wasn't just a story. It was a reality still written on the landscape.

Out there away from the towns and cities there was no escaping the reality that Australia had belonged to the Indigenous people, and in some sense it always would. Every rock and every seep of water had its story, like a title deed. Then men and women like her forebears had come in and taken it all for themselves. In 1959 that wasn't something people talked about, but from then on whenever our family went for a picnic to some glorious bit of bush she'd look around and say, This must have been paradise for the Aborigines before we came along. It was her way of acknowledging what she'd learned in the Centre, and of trying to make us aware of it too.

She wrote a piece about her trip, planning to send it to a magazine. Among her papers there are several drafts in which you can sense her trying to process an experience too deep to be immediately understood. There's no final copy and it was never published. Going to the Centre had been a life-changing experience, but not one that she could find the right words for.

She brought back a few souvenirs: a small piece of the Rock, a rough boomerang that she'd seen return to the hand of the man who'd thrown it, a matchbox full of red dirt, and a book of 'Dreamtime Stories' retold for children. She was upset that I found those stories dull. Now I see that she was trying to share what she'd experienced.

Years later she and I were clearing out a cupboard and came across the piece of Uluru, a small shard of rough red stone that seemed still warm from the sun. We both knew it should go back to where it belonged. We didn't go so far as to return it to Uluru, but we went out to the bush and laid it on the ground under a tree. I often think of it there, under rain and sun, the mark of two people blundering towards some kind of understanding.

Dolly came to live with us for good when I was about five. I remember her as a thin, cranky, frightening old woman. I never saw her smile.

Her years of smoking finally caught up with her and at the end of 1959 she died. The complicated relationship Nance had always had with her—part war, part love, all longing—was caught in the inscription she chose for her mother's plaque. It was just one word: PAX. Peace, of course. Under that, like a note so deep only some ears might hear it, was the idea of truce and, behind that, forgiveness.

Bert went on living alone at Green Hills into his eighties. Then one day he was out in the paddock and the sheep he was holding was struck by lightning. The sheep more or less evaporated and Bert was knocked unconscious. When he came to, he went inside and made a cup of tea. Ken joked that even the Almighty couldn't finish him off, but it was a sign that the old man couldn't go on forever at the farm.

When he came to live with us, one of the things he brought with him was the pair of sheep shears that had made him, in his young days, a gun shearer. He brought them out one day to show me: dull grey metal, all one piece, oiled and wrapped in a bit of cloth. His huge hands effortlessly closed and opened the blades. When I tried, even using both hands, the sprung steel was too strong for me. I couldn't imagine how you'd bend over a sheep, lock it between your knees, and slice those blades through the fleece for hour after hour.

Dolly and Bert were as strange to me as if they were from another planet. They made my mother strange to me too. This scary old woman and this big rough old man were her mother and father, but there was no way to put my Latin-using, poetry-quoting mother together with these old people with their foreign ways.

Nance had just turned fifty when she started an arts degree, majoring in French and Italian. At first the university course was for the sake of the study itself. She'd given herself a home-made education in English literature. Now, with old age and death around the corner, she wanted to discover the mighty works of human understanding that lay locked behind other languages. She was looking for a way to find meaning. Not in God and the carrot-and-stick of the afterlife, but in grasping the hand of another spirit who'd travelled the same path. Death was still at the end of that path. But, through art, you died having had full consciousness of your life.

Her first assignment in French was to write a one-page essay, *L'histoire de ma vie*. She told me she laughed aloud when the lecturer wrote the title on the blackboard and everyone turned to look at this old woman laughing at the idea of putting her fifty years on one page. Her essay came back embroidered all over with remarks in tiny red writing. '*Environ* is based on a pleonastic and slovenly use of *about*: if you say *about five* it is idle to add *or six*, because six is about five.' She was ready to give up, thought she'd left it too late to learn. Then she realised the young girl next to her was in tears. Her essay was almost hidden under the mass of scornful little red words. Nance pushed her own paper along so the girl could see. Nice new red pen, she said. He wanted to get his money's worth.

I've still got some of her French and Italian texts in which, against all the rules she'd been taught, she wrote in the margins. *Le Lac: new attitude towards Nature. New element is movement, flowing H_2O*. Her thumbed copy of *Les Fleurs du mal* is thick with her comments. Beside those famous lines *Là, tout n'est qu'ordre et beauté, / Luxe, calme et volupté* she's written: *Here as opposed to there reign disorder, ugliness, poverty, restlessness and pain. Poet has to suffer but his words will live on.*

In Molière she found a grittier, wittier fellowship. When one of Molière's self-deluding characters— a would-be writer—says modestly that he hopes his style is fine enough, she recognised another writer closer to home. Her note here is in the tiniest writing, as if her husband might overhear: *Yes, very happy picture of a proud author.*

In the same way that she'd memorised Keats and Shakespeare and made them her own, she learned by heart the famous opening of Dante's *Inferno*:

> *Nel mezzo del cammin di nostra vita,*
> *mi ritrovai per una selva oscura,*
> *ché la diritta via era smarrita.*
>
> *(In the middle of the journey of our life,*
> *I found myself in a dark wood,*
> *where the straight path was lost.)*

Of all the writers she studied, Proust spoke to her most personally. Here was a dying man, racing against illness to get his great work done, because in the shadow cast by mortality he had to confront the biggest question of all, the same one she'd dimly grasped the night she'd decided not to step in front of the Enmore tram. His answer was that if life was the wound, art was its healer, because art was the wound shared.

Partly in the hope of improving her accent, and partly to leave a house where her husband was often suspiciously absent, Nance made her first trip to France in 1965. She was fifty-three. She did a short course at the Sorbonne. Her letters were exhilarated, full of ever-so-casual French. *I had to go this morning to Boul'Mich near the Sorbonne and buy d'occasion a formidable looking grammar... The city here is still covered with snow, it has turned to ice on the trottoirs...*

She'd nearly finished her degree when the marriage that had lasted for nearly twenty-five years came to an end. Ken was involved with another woman and she was pregnant. Nance had thought that she and Ken had arrived at an arrangement where each of them could live their own lives, within the bond created by their years together. Now, approaching sixty, she was alone.

Among her papers I found an envelope where she'd jotted down something she must have read somewhere. *L'amour et le travail: if the first is lacking you have only to redouble the second.* The arts degree became more than a hobby. She saw that it could offer her a whole new life. She did an honours year, then a teaching diploma and a diploma in teaching English as a foreign language. Forty years after her mother had stopped her, Nance became a teacher. She taught French in schools, taught English to newly arrived migrant children, and ran her own business teaching English to the wives of Japanese businessmen.

She travelled to Europe several more times, never as a tourist but always in the spirit of the pilgrim.

One of her last trips was to Florence, where she stood in front of the frescoes that Dante had seen. A line came into her mind from somewhere in all her reading: *Suffering pierces the shield of habit.* It was a thought that made sense of the unhappiness she'd known, and also the happiness. She knew that ultimately it didn't matter what happened to you. In the light of eternity, in the light of all those dead writers in whose work she'd recognised the great truths, only one thing mattered. What other people did was up to them. Your job was to live—as richly and honestly as you could—your one life.

Nance wrote a letter that was attached to her will. It started:

> *My dear children,*
> *First, I want to say, you children have made my life,*
> *you are the only important thing I ever did and I want*
> *to thank you for all you have given me. Each of you is*
> *special and each of you is different which I regard as a*
> *great good. I'm like the Roman matron who said of her*
> *children: 'These are my jewels.'*

What a great gift it was to have had her for a mother. From the solid base of the love she gave us, all three of us discovered lives of fulfilment: Christopher as a barrister, Stephen as an economist, and me, after a slow start, as a writer.

Why does a person become a writer? I owe so much to my mother. She read to me when I was a child, made it clear how much literature mattered, told me the family stories that, years later, inspired the books I'm most proud of having written. When I was suddenly bored with children's books she handed me *The Blush and Other Stories* by Elizabeth Taylor, and a new world of adult behaviour and beautiful writing was opened up to my half-comprehending twelve-year-old mind. When I began to write, she was supportive and encouraging in the most practical ways. One or two mornings a week I'd take our two young children to her house. She'd have made me a cut lunch and a thermos, as she'd done when I was at school. Then I'd drive to a nearby park and get into the back seat with one of the kids' boogie boards across my lap for a desk. For a few hours I'd have the luxury she never did: time to get on with my own work, knowing the children were having a richly enjoyable time with their loving granny.

If someone had done all that for Nance Russell, might she have become a writer rather than the most engaged of readers? It's more than possible. The memoir-fragments she left are mostly matter-of-fact, but now and then there's a quick blaze of something more expressive. The diary she kept irregularly in her later years is full of pungent observations about the people around her. But, apart from that letter to the newspaper about prunes, she was never published. Luck and life circumstances are often all that makes the difference between someone who writes and someone who doesn't, and—like so many women of her generation—she wasn't favoured with either.

Ken knew more about the difficulties of the writing life than Nance, but he also encouraged me when I chose that path. He had three books published—a novel called *A Maid from Heaven* in 1965, a non-fiction book about the Vietnam War in 1972, and a memoir of his Trotskyite days in 2006. I was fifteen when the galleys arrived for the novel: long narrow coils of slippery paper that I helped him proofread. It was fascinating to see how the physical object of a book was arrived at, and it was a new idea that a published writer could be someone as ordinary as the father I saw every day buttering his toast and making bad puns.

I was on the last drafts of this book and full of doubts about it when, by a series of lucky chances, I met Ria Murch ('Not diarrhoea, not gonorrhoea, just Ria'). She was a great age and, as she put it, on and off like a light bulb on the blink. I asked her, Ria, do you remember my mother Nance Gee?

Her face—still like a mischievous pixie's despite the ravages of age—blossomed into a huge smile. Oh, she said, your mother was a *remarkable* woman! The switch blinked off, but that brilliant flash of memory was a reminder of why it was worth trying to tell Nance's story.

Writing about a real person, especially your own mother, is difficult. Unlike characters in fiction, real people's motives are muddled and obscure, their personalities seem to shift from one day to another, and their lives are full of events that come out of nowhere. Thinking about your mother as a woman, with a private inner life, is daunting. It can feel as if you shouldn't go there.

Still, this book is my attempt to continue what our mother wanted to achieve with those fragments of memoir: to tell her story and put it in its context of time and place. I hope it might be something like the book she might have written, if she'd ever had the right pencil.

ACKNOWLEDGMENTS

MY FIRST and warmest thanks go to Ste and Ly—all those cups of excellent coffee and the warm welcome you both gave me over the long process of writing this book were so much appreciated.

I also thank the many others who were so generous with their time, knowledge, and memories. Among them were members of the extended families of Wisemans, Russells, Maunders, and Gees—thank you for sharing your family stories with me. I'm so grateful to others whose parents, uncles or aunts knew my mother and who allowed me to use part of their own story to enrich mine. Thank you to all those who shared their knowledge and resources of old-time pharmacy with me, and the many librarians, archivists, local historians and others who went to such trouble to help me in my effort to understand and visualise the past. I'm very grateful to the friends who read parts of drafts and gave me insightful suggestions.

A remarkable series of serendipities gave me the opportunity to talk with two men who'd been on The Line with Uncle Frank. It was a privilege and a great pleasure to meet Sir John Carrick and the late Wal Ward, and hear their memories of 'Russ'.

Thank you, Lisa Allen, Barrie Anthony, Bessie Bardwell, Helena Berenson, Suzanne Bryce, Campbelltown and Airds Historical Society, Campbelltown Public School Archives, Mary Coupe, Jean Debelle and family, Lorraine Evison, Suzanne Falkiner, Christine Frater, Jennifer Freeman, Lloyd Gledhill, Tony Gledhill, Hall School Museum, Susan Hampton, Jan Ho, Kristy-Lee Hyder, Mrs Molly Keane, Nita Kieg, Deborah Kingsland, Danny Kingsley, Glenda Korporaal, Ku-ring-gai Historical Society, Curtis Levy, Ross Lane, Bill Larkin, Judy McDonald, John Mackie, my webmaster Col Madden, Julia Mant, Don Maunder, Helen Maxwell, Tom Molomby, Deirdre and Ivor Morton, Michelle and John Murch, Moffatt Oxenbould, the late Ernie Ranclaud, Marita Ranclaud, Anna Rigg, David Roberts, John and Deborah Russell, Meg Sadler, Edna Saunders, Paul Serov, Susanna Short, Anne Stevens, St George Girls' High Archives, Temora Historical Society, Tamworth Historical Society, and Lee Whitmore.

Thanks also to my agent Barbara Mobbs, a trustworthy voice of good sense in all the uncertainties of writing a book.

In spite of all the help I had in writing this book, and my best efforts, there are sure to be errors. I apologise in advance, and will appreciate being put right.

A MOTHER'S LIFE

How to Collect Your Mother's Story

MUM LOVED to tell the stories of her young life. All through my childhood she told me over and over again the stories about the grand hotel her father had owned and then lost, and her miserable apprentice days at the Enmore pharmacy.

I tended to glaze over when Mum started in again about the Caledonian and the pharmacy. (My punishment is to see the same look on the faces of my own children.) The trouble is, the ones with the memories want people to hear them, and those others often don't want to listen – until suddenly they do, and it's too late. How many readers of this book have come up to me and said, oh, if only I'd asked my mother more about her life! If only I'd got her to write some of it down!

I was lucky that Mum lived long enough for me to see the value of the stories she had to tell. But why does it take so long, and how can we catch those stories before it's too late?

Growing up means growing away from our parents: we have to work out how to separate ourselves from them as well as love them. While we're doing that, perhaps we can't afford to be too interested in their stories. We're busy making our own.

I was in my late thirties when I realised that the stories I only half-remembered from Mum were precious. They were a very personal link backwards – not history from a textbook but from the felt experience of someone who'd lived through it.

They were also a way of evolving a new kind of relationship with my mother. I'd always just thought of her as 'Mum'; now I was ready to get to know her as a woman. Partly, it was having children of my own. Mostly, though, it was because I'd got to the stage of life where I knew at first-hand the things she'd talked about: falling in love, being jilted, doing the jilting myself, having a career, making a choice about a life partner.

'Just write down all those stories you've told me about your life, Mum,' I urged her. I didn't realise then how hard it is to do something that seems so simple.

My thirty-year-old son asked me the other day if I'd write down a few things about my life, and when I tried to oblige I realised how hard it is.

Part of the resistance is the difficulty in believing that any of it is interesting enough. I think that's especially a problem for women. Even if we have satisfying careers, the heart of our emotional lives is often the home and family. In our society, that dimension of life is usually regarded as secondary to the things that really matter: politics, war, grand achievements.

Also, no one likes to be thought of as a narcissist. As women we're still trying to sort out how to be assertive without being aggressive; how to value ourselves without putting tickets on ourselves. It all makes it hard to sit down and write about *me, me, me.*

Writing things down can be hard; the inner school-marm can get activated and we get hung up on where to start, and how do you spell 'accommodation'? There are few things more daunting than a blank page or screen, and the silence of the room waiting for you to write something fascinating.

One way to prime the pump is to invent a listener – to write in the form of a letter, perhaps to a child or grandchild. That way, the writing is more like a conversation than a school exercise, and it's easier to let yourself jump around from one story to another, and tell the story in your own way, in your own words.

But it's often easier for the stories to get told in the course of an actual conversation. Get a cup of tea going, get the family photo album out, and open it to the first page. 'Now, who on earth is that?' If there's an audio recorder sitting among the tea cups, it will soon be forgotten. An interested listener makes such a difference; suddenly the stories come to life with the kind of specifics that mightn't appear in a starchier written version:

the embarrassing details of being caught without a train ticket, the juiciness of those stolen apples, exactly what Billy said when you broke his tennis racquet.

Talking also means the story sounds like a person. A written account will be inclined to be formal, over-correct, all about the events and the information. A conversation will have all the turns of phrase, the choice of words and above all the feelings of a real flesh-and-blood person.

So what happens to those stories once they've been written or recorded? Family histories take many forms, and they're all good. Some can remain just as they come from the pen or mouth of the person who told them: others might be typed up and edited a little – put into chronological order, repetitions removed, ramblings compressed. Some are just the facts, others are embellished with research. Some get embellished so far they turn into fiction.

Some – perhaps most – are just for the family. But sometimes there's an urge to see them go public, and then things can get complicated. Digging into family pasts can uncover things people would rather stay hidden. People remember events differently. They disagree about what picture should be shown to the world.

Writers have differing views about how to deal with this. Some feel the story has to be told, no matter what. My own feeling is that a family story is jointly owned and if it's published, all the people involved need to be happy with it. Sometimes it's enough to change a few names and details, or leave out the most controversial parts. In extreme cases, a family story might have to be put away in a drawer until it can no longer hurt anyone.

Every life is about the choices made within the opportunities available. That means they're all interesting and all worth recording. But they're fragile treasures. It only takes one generation failing to pass them on, and they're gone from the world as completely as the dodo. Saving family stories from extinction is a thing richly worth doing. You gain a new perspective on yourself and your place in the larger world. Best of all, you know you're leaving something that will be valued by the ones who come after.

A few tips to get started

If you're encouraging someone to write down their stories, don't give them a special, brand-new, fancy book. It will be hard to live up to it and they'll feel every word has to be brilliant. Suggest they use an old exercise book or just loose sheets of paper.

If they're using some kind of audio recorder, make it a simple one so they can just press the button when they think of something, rather than sitting down for an official recording session with complicated technology. A phone is good (and a grandchild might enjoy showing them how to record on it).

Encourage them not to worry about starting at the beginning – just get the stories down in whatever order they remember them – it will be easy enough to put them in order later.

If you're going to record a conversation and ask a few questions, make it just the two of you – a three-way conversation gets a bit busy, especially for an older person.

Ask as few questions as possible. You might have to weather a bit of rambling, but that's better than closing everything down by being too directive. Open-ended questions are best – not so much 'What year was that?' but 'How did you meet (whoever)?', 'What was the worst/best thing about (whatever)?', 'What did (the place) look like?'

Good triggers for memories might be photos, old family objects, mention of a place, a person, a pet, a particular pair of shoes, a family joke . . .

Family stories are partly about the 'What happened?' but they're also about capturing the feel of the people. The events and dates can often be found elsewhere, but the individuality of the people can't. A family story doesn't have to be about big or historically important things: it's often the seemingly trivial stories that bring a person or a moment to life. As someone helping to record a family story, you don't have to be a historian. Let the conversation follow its own course – bring it gently back to the story if it goes too far away, but the most vivid and unique stories will come from a relaxed mood. Keep the cups of tea and chocolate biscuits coming!

CANON▮▮GATE.tv

CHANNELLING GREAT CONTENT

 WATCH — INTERVIEWS, TRAILERS, ANIMATIONS, READINGS, GIGS

 LISTEN — AUDIO BOOKS, PODCASTS, MUSIC, PLAYLISTS

 READ — CHAPTERS, EXCERPTS, SNEAK PEEKS, RECOMMENDATIONS

 DISCOVER — BLOGS, EVENTS, NEWS, CREATIVE PARTNERS

 SHOP — LIMITED EDITIONS, BUNDLES, SECRET SALES